SOCCER DRILLS FOR INDIVIDUAL AND TEAM PLAY

Soccer Drills for Individual and Team Play

James P. McGettigan

PRENTICE HALL
Englewood Cliffs, New Jersey 07632

Prentice-Hall International (UK) Limited, *London*
Prentice-Hall of Australia Pty. Limited, *Sydney*
Prentice-Hall Canada, Inc., *Toronto*
Prentice-Hall Hispanoamericana, S.A., *Mexico*
Prentice-Hall of India Private Limited, *New Delhi*
Prentice-Hall of Japan, Inc., *Tokyo*
Simon & Schuster Asia Pte. Ltd., *Singapore*
Editora Prentice-Hall do Brasil., Ltda., *Rio de Janeiro*

© 1987 *by*

PRENTICE-HALL, INC.
Englewood Cliffs, NJ

10 9 8 7 6 5 4 3

10 9 8 7 6   PBK

Library of Congress Cataloging-in-Publication Data

McGettigan, James P.
  Soccer drills for individual and team play.

  Includes index.
  1. Soccer—Training. 2. Soccer—Coaching.
I. Title.
GV943.9.T7M33   1986   796.334'07'7   86-22529

ISBN 0-13-815309-4

ISBN 0-13-815366-3 {PBK}

PRENTICE HALL
BUSINESS & PROFESSIONAL DIVISION
A division of Simon & Schuster
Englewood Cliffs, New Jersey 07632

Printed in the United States of America

Acknowledgments

First and foremost, thanks to those who continue to improve upon all that we already know about the game of soccer. Much of their efforts are included in this book.

Throughout the world, coaches borrow, beg, and steal ideas from each other to develop their own methods and philosophies. For this reason, I extend a special thanks to those individuals who have contributed to the development of my methods and philosophy. Any success I have achieved is directly related to their efforts.

This book would not be possible without the expert skills of Barbara McGettigan and William Hamilton. Barbara, my wife, thanks for the long hours spent on the diagrams that appear in this book and Bill, thanks for your editorial advice.

Contents

How to Get the Most Out of This Book

This book can be an aid for the beginner, intermediate, and advanced soccer coach. The beginner coach can attain an overall view of the job he has undertaken, to develop a team. The intermediate coach can use this book to add to the methods he has chosen to develop his team. The advanced coach can use it as a supplementary aid. It can help a coach to be more effective and efficient in his approach to coaching.

I recognize that there are many methods used in training soccer players and that drills are created and revised every day. There is no reason a coach cannot revise any of the drills from this book.

I am not advocating that a coach use all the drills in this book. A coach should use the drills that serve his needs and not become too complicated in his approach. I am a firm believer in keeping it simple. It is better to attempt to know a few drills well than attempt to know numerous drills in a less than adequate manner.

I have seen teams whose only "set" maneuver used during a game was a wall pass, but they did it, and did it so well that they ran circles around their opponents. Nevertheless, soccer has improved tremendously in the United States. It is time to move ahead and learn more tactical maneuvers and drills and above all, to learn them well.

THE ADVANTAGES OF A WIDE VARIETY OF DRILLS

Many training programs are geared to fit the needs of the outstanding or ideal player. However, how many coaches actually have eleven players that can carry out such a program? Consequently, coaches try to use an ideal program that falls short because their players lack the ability, experience, intelligence, maturity, and skill level required. For this reason, this book provides coaches with a wide variety of drills and methods to choose from to fit their specific personnel.

Success in soccer coaching depends a great deal on talent. But what about those teams that do not have an abundance of talent, yet are still consistently successful despite their shortcomings? If you were to examine the preparation of such teams, you would probably find drills that strongly emphasize fundamental skills and tactics. Also, you would probably find a team that gets progressively better as the season goes on and a team that wins against teams with far superior talent. The coach of such a team is not a magician. He is simply a person who has carefully done his homework. In his practice sessions he uses repetitive drills to hone and refine players' skills. He is the type of coach who recognizes that, "Rome wasn't built in a day." In other words, he is patient, he is organized, and he is methodical. He is aware that whatever happens in a game can be improved through hard work and practice. Normally when things go wrong in match play, he says to himself, "What can I do in the practice session that will help my team to improve its situation?" Next, he sets up drills that his players will understand. His practice sessions concentrate on structuring habits and reactions that directly relate to improving what happens in match play.

HOW DO DRILLS FIT INTO A SOCCER TRAINING PROGRAM?

The first task of a soccer coach is to have in his mind or on paper a general plan for improving all phases of the game of soccer for his players. These phases of training include technique, tactics, fitness, and a system of play.

During the general improvement stages of technique, tactics, and fitness, a coach can establish a clear idea of the strengths and weaknesses of his players. Once he has established what his strengths and weaknesses are he can begin the second phase of training, which is to reinforce his strengths and to minimize or eliminate his weaknesses. There are drills in this book that can be used for the first phase of training or the general phase to discover weaknesses, and also drills for the second phase of training to reinforce the team's strengths and eliminate or minimize the team's weaknesses.

Most coaches go through this process to develop a team for playing soccer.

Systems of play, meaning how players are arranged or stationed on the field during the game, are determined when a coach observes his players' abilities during phase one and phase two of the training program. In other words, a system of play is determined by the caliber of the players that a coach is training.

Drills are a fundamental means of improving a team's shortcomings. When a coach witnesses incorrect execution, verbal correction is rarely enough to ensure that his team will not repeat its mistakes. Consequently, he must analyze the error situation, break it down into understandable parts, and develop a drill that will promote a proper execution. He must then reinforce learning by further repetition.

HOW THIS BOOK IS ORGANIZED

The format used in this book covers most areas of training players for match play.

The four sections are:

1. Skill Drills
2. Basic Patterns
3. Special Situations
4. Training Games

Each of the four sections of this book has an overall major objective.

The major objective of the performing skill drills section is to acquire a specific skill, such as: heading, passing, controlling, and so forth. Rarely is a single skill performed by itself. Therefore, skills should be learned in a combined state, such as: trapping and passing; trapping-turning and dribbling off; and so on. The closer a combination of skills approaches one integrated skill, the more effectively it can be used in match play. A well-skilled player saves time through proficient execution of skills and, as a result, he is able to use open space more advantageously than a less-skilled player.

The major objective of performing basic pattern drills is to enable players in small groups to become proficient at performing basic skills in a predetermined pattern. The drills enable players to move a ball at the opportune moment toward a goal in a sensible, efficient manner.

The major objective of special situation drills is to take advantage of special situations that occur during a game, such as corner crossing plays, corner kick plays, throw-in plays, and penalty kicks.

In the training games section, the major objective is to involve players in training games, which emphasize various techniques and tactics that might be missed in a practice session, unless they are specifically planned. An example of this type of activity is playing soccer in a "one-touch."

Certain sections of this book concentrate on activities that improve technique and organic fitness. Specific time should be earmarked in a practice session in these areas of preparation. It is important that a coach have a wide variety of activities to choose from to prepare players and also to prevent boredom in the practice session.

Remember that no one training system will fit the needs of every coach. Coaches' training needs are different because their players possess different levels of skill development, tactical knowledge, and physical fitness. For these reasons it is absurd to recommend that a coach follow any book verbatim. A coach should pick out the drills that serve his needs and, in addition, he should modify them to best fit his particular needs.

The drills in this book can be used to enhance a coach's own collection of training drills. Even if a coach uses only a handful of these drills it should be worth the price he paid for his book.

The drills and games included in this book come from many sources: those I've devised, those devised by players on my team and by other coaches, and those found in books, movies, and clinches. Some of these drills and games may be used on a daily basis or in special situations, as circumstances demand.

BACKGROUND INFORMATION RELATING TO DRILL EXECUTION

The following questions and answers should be considered before setting up a drill program because it is important professionally to know "why" as well as "how".

Why Use Drills?

Repetition in small groups produces economical, efficient learning.

How Will Drills and Small Group Games Improve Team Play?

A team that is better able to meet the challenges of small group encounters is more successful in the outcome of match play because it is better able to handle the numerical advantage situations.

What Are Steps for Teaching a Drill?

There are seven basic steps:

1. introduce the drill
2. demonstrate the drill
3. explore the parts of the drill
4. organize the players into performing groups
5. have the players execute the drill
6. correct mistakes and reinforce proper execution
7. have the players practice until learning is evident

What Are the Key Principles for Effective Drills?

General Principles and Execution Principles: general principles involve background knowledge and understanding relating indirectly to the drilling process. Execution principles relate directly to the process of carrying out the drill.

General Principles

No drill is worth much unless it specifically relates to what happens in a game of soccer.

Players should be made aware of how the drill relates to the game of soccer.

Drills should not take up more than a quarter of the practice session, unless a special need for more time is evident. Remember, drilling is only part of a practice session.

Drills should be introduced at a slow pace; the performance speed can be gradually increased as learning occurs.

Drills should be modified to accommodate the physical fitness, age, and the abilities of the players.

Drills should be set up to cover all phases of soccer play, that is the areas of defense, midfield, and attack.

Drills should be kept simple and should be easily understood.

A long-range plan should be developed so that players will receive several kinds of experience from a variety of drills.

Drills should be used extensively during the preseason and early season. In mid and late season they can be used as the need develops.

Drills should move from the simple to the complex. Drills should first be performed without defenders, then against defenders.

Drills should be modified to meet each specific team's needs.

Drills should not be permitted to become monotonous. A variety of drills will help to keep player interest at a high level.

As fatigue sets in, technique deteriorates and the quality of learning becomes impaired. To combat this condition frequent rest periods are recommended. If initial attempts at a drill fail, persistence will pay off. Also, if enthusiasm about the value of drills is shown, it will usually spread to the players.

The objective of drilling is to make the players perform automatically when confronted with a similar situation in match play.

Execution Principles:

Review the drill procedure before a practice session and make sure you know how it works. Be prepared.

When introducing a new drill, walk one group of players through it so that the other players can see how it should be performed.

Avoid talking too much. Get the players into action. Players learn by doing.

Break the drill down into key steps or key words that will help players remember the drill sequence. For example: passing order—1 "through," 2 "back," 3 "square."

Involve as many players as possible in the drill and don't allow players to just stand around and watch. Instead, keep the players active.

When tactical or technical errors occur interrupt the drill momentarily to correct the error.

Provide for lanes of traffic that will not interfere with the drill in progress.

Praise groups that carry the drill out well, and encourage groups having difficulties.

Caution players about unnecessary roughness, carelessness, or dangerous practices.

If a drill calls for boundary lines, insist the players stay inside them.

If equipment (flags, cones, etc.) is necessary, have it set up beforehand.

Don't put all the good players in one group. Distribute them evenly so that others can benefit from their example.

If a defensive and offensive rule is required in a drill, make sure players get a chance to experience both.

Insist on good technique and accuracy.

Provide for a system of ball collecting. For example: after a shot on goal, each player should collect his own ball.

When a drill calls for a pass on the ground, insist that it be passed on the ground.

When a drill calls for "1-touch" plays or left foot only, insist that players conform.

In grid drills, the smaller the restricted area, the greater the pressure will be to maintain ball control.

Encourage players to use feints to conceal their intentions while drilling.

What Are the Steps Used to Develop a Team for Match Play?

To prepare for a soccer season, a coach needs an organizational plan. This plan should include specific and general objectives concerning the preseason, the season, and the post season programs.

Daily programs with specific drills on technique, tactics, and fitness activities are the basis for preparing for the season. Drills for daily programs are classified as either basic skill development, pressure, or functional drills.

Basic skill development drills include the learning and practice of rote skills such as passing, heading, trapping, and so forth.

Pressure drills are used to refine and reinforce basic skills, the performer is put under pressure by making him repeat a skill or skills at a rapid rate. For example: a player is placed inside the center circle, six other players are stationed outside the center circle. Each of the players outside the circle has a ball. In turn, the players outside the circle rapidly serve balls to the player in the center of the circle. He traps the ball and immediately sends it back to the outside player that passed it to him. Then the inside player moves to the next player on the outside of the circle and continues the same drill. This is all done at a rapid rate so that the player in the center of the circle is kept under constant pressure to receive and to pass back. When players show improvement, opponents can be introduced to the drill to add further pressure.

Functional training centers around the position a player chooses or is assigned to by the coach. Skills and tactics are performed in the position assigned and in the area of the field that the tactic or skill will most likely be used. For example, two strikers and a mid-field player should practice passing to get a shot at the goal while in the vicinity of the goal. Functional training drills can be performed with or without opponents. In fact, it is best that they be performed first without opponents. Initially the attacking team is given numerical advantage, and, as progress is indicated, more opponents should be introduced to the drills.

Each of these three types of drills should be introduced at a specific time during a season. Early in a season basic skill development should be used extensively. Next pressure drills should be introduced, and finally functional drills should become a major focal point.

Even though each type of drill has a specific time to be used during a season, a coach must be flexible in his approach. This is true because of diverse skill levels, age variations, and varying degrees of experience. If a coach finds his players skill development to be high, he may not need to spend as much time on basic skills. He can then go on to pressure drills and come back to skill drills only as the need arises or as is indicated by his players performance in pressure drills or functional drills. A further indication of the type of drills needed can come from player's performance in scrimmage games or actual match play.

As all training systems have good points and bad points, no one training system can solve all problems. Therefore, a coach's initial starting effort should be to practice basic skills and to work on the players' physical conditioning.

Next, the coach may continue training by using the grid system, which is a valuable tool early in the training season and becomes less so as the season progresses.

Once a team has mastered maneuvers in the squares, it is time to move on the fluid or movement drills. In these drills, players perform maneuvers and patterns while moving down the field.

The practice can then move to small-group tactics, which include traditional passing patterns such as the wall pass, give and go, scissors, back passes, overlapping, screening, and decoying. These passing patterns have proven to be effective methods of moving the ball.

Finally, direct practice toward improving both offensive and defensive play by working with a group of players within the team, such as wing and mid-field players or a goalkeeper and two defenders. Direct practice toward a group of players who by virtue of their positions work together in a game situation.

Ultimately, team practice is centered around the scrimmage. During the scrimmage, interrupt play in order to point out situations and plays that should or should not have occurred. Also interrupt to introduce special plays and situations such as a penalty kick, goal kicks, or a kickoff situation. At this point, the team should be practicing small-group tactics in order to emphasize, correct, and reinforce a segment of the team that needs attention.

No matter what system of progression is used to prepare a team for match play, this book, whether used as an integral part or in a supplementary manner, will fit into a coach's plan to accomplish this end.

I

SKILL DRILLS

SKILLS

Where should a soccer coach start in developing his team for the coming season? Any coach will tell you the answer is in the improvement of skills and techniques. However, along with this skill development, a coach can improve the physical fitness of the players as well. Physical fitness complements skill development in that it enables a player to perform skills at a high rate of speed over prolonged periods. Even though skill development and physical fitness can occur at the same time, skill development is the first major objective in the early part of a soccer season. Physical fitness, on the other hand, is progressively developed throughout the entire year or season.

Soccer skills are best learned in progressive steps. Skills are initially performed at a slow pace from a stationary position; then they are performed at a trotting pace; and finally running. Further progression is the performance of skills with the resistance of an opponent first with one-half resistance, then three-fourths resistance, and finally with full pressure from an opponent.

Once a skill or technique is learned, it is then reinforced by repetition. Repetition enables a player to execute his skills at a high rate of speed, which is essential in a game situation. Players will then be able to perform the skills quickly without having to consciously think about each segment of the skill.

Certain skills are interrelated, such as: passing, receiving, and controlling the ball. As these skills are interrelated, they should be combined in the training process once the separate skills are learned. These developing skills are included in the first chapter because of their importance in developing effective teamwork and in keeping possession of the ball.

All team players should participate in the skill drills in the first five chapters with the exception of the goalkeeper. Goalkeeper skill drills are found in Chapter 6. Development of a wide range

3

of skills acquired from participating in these skill drills will definitely help a player when participating in match play.

Why should a coach use drills rather than a scrimmage setting to teach skills? Learning physical skills requires a combination of inherited abilities. These abilities include coordination, balance, speed, reaction time, and so forth.

The majority of physical skills cannot be learned on a one-time try basis. Therefore some type of repetitive training is necessary for learning physical or motor skills. A skilled performer rarely consciously thinks about the parts of a complete skill when he is performing. Yet this same person, when he was learning specific skills, did more thinking about the parts of a complete skill. The learning process is completed when he does not have to think of each segment of his skills and he performs the skills well. This does not mean that he is not required to concentrate and anticipate, for the initiation of the whole skill requires concentration and anticipation.

For the above reasons, it is logical to be an advocate of using repetition, a habit-forming process in learning physical skills.

An individual who learns his skills in match play or in scrimmages may overlook correcting his bad habits for the sake of immediate expediency. It is difficult for a coach to change a bad habit that has been reinforced through the years. Many times this individual has been reasonably successful in his performance and he is reluctant to change. Yet, this same individual could have learned his skills and refined these skills in a drill setting designed to weed out poor habits and incorrect performance responses. All things being equal, the individual who refined his skills in a drill process has a better chance for self improvement.

Every sport has its own movements and skills that are unique to that sport. All sports require certain common movements, but, more important, each sport has movement that is unique to itself. For example, a basketball player and a soccer player need to be able to run, feint, change their paces. The skills necessary to play these two sports differ, so there should be a different emphasis in the training of these athletes. Specific muscle groups that need developing differ within these two sports.

It is not only necessary to learn a skill but to learn how this skill is used or fits into a game situation. Rote skill should be put into game usage as soon as possible. It is important for a player to know how rote skill is used and integrated with his other skills and with the skills of his teammates.

Attaining a high degree of skill in soccer enables each player to do two things:

1. Use these skills to personally overcome difficulties that opponents throw in front of him.
2. Use these skills to be able to work efficiently with his teammates to overcome opponents.

There are times in a game when a player must use his skills and work by himself. On more frequent occasions, a player in a game needs his skills to work with his teammates, to defend, and to attack. Each player needs to be encouraged to develop both types of skills.

Certain factors should be considered when alloting time for skill drills, such as the time available, length of the season, and the length of the practice session. Furthermore, the age, physical condition, and players' skill level ability all have a bearing on the time assigned to these areas of preparation.

During the early season training program, coaches should spend a maximum time in practicing skill drills. But as the season progresses, less time should be alloted to these skill drills unless a specific need is evident.

Individual players can always contribute to a team effort by sharpening their individual and group skills and techniques. The skills in this book can help you and your team to attain this goal.

1

Passing, Receiving, and Controlling

The mechanics of the modern game of soccer are centered around three skills—passing, receiving, and controlling. These skills are interrelated and therefore should be practiced and refined together. They are necessary for effective team work and for maintaining possession of the ball and are the means by which the attacking team moves a ball toward a goal. Furthermore, these skills are the means by which the attacking team establishes numerical superiority in the vicinity of the ball.

Players should be prepared to be effective with a wide range of passing, receiving, and controlling skills. They should be able to make short passes, medium passes, and long passes with accuracy and, in many occasions, with power. By the same token, they should be able to receive and control these passes.

The greater percentage of passes in a game are short passes and therefore more time should be assigned to developing these abilities. This does not mean that we should neglect practicing long passing because long passes are very important in switching play from one side of the field to the other, in attacking, and in counter-attacking. However, as ball possession is very important in the modern game, it is better accomplished with the short pass.

Ideally, the game of soccer should be played in a "1-touch"

fashion. This is not a reality or practicality because very few, if any, players can develop the skill necessary to play a "1-touch" game. During match play, players are constantly in motion. Chances for effective passes appear and disappear at a rapid rate. A player must sometimes hold a ball, keep possession of it, and wait for a safer time to pass. Recognizing human inadequacies, we must use the second best way to play the game and that is with "2-touch" or with multiple touches. Whenever possible, however, players should be reminded to go back and use the "1-touch" system when practical.

Good players can make a "2-touch" skill look like a "1 touch" skill. They move toward the ball, take a ball out of the air, turn their body and pass the ball off in one motion with each skill flowing into the other. It's quick, and needs to be so, because today's game requires this type of skill. Constant defensive pressure dictates that we move the ball quickly or it will be lost to the opponents. Quick control enables a team to perform without panicking. It enables players to gain the time needed to assess the situation, to pass off, or to shoot at the goal. A basic objective of the defensive player is to rush the attacker and to hurry his actions so he will make mistakes. The responsibility of effective ball control lies not only with the receiver but also with the passer. A player contributes very little when he spins the ball off to another player when he could have just as easily sent an on the ground, crisp pass.

It is difficult to write about passing, receiving, and controlling without referring to support play. What is the responsibility of the player who is in the area of the ball, although he does not have possession of it? Many spectators only see what happens with the person in control of the ball. They have their eyes glued on the ball. They recognize a good shot or a good pass but they have very little awareness of what happens to make the pass or shot possible. The untrained eye sees a forward break out and rush toward a goal and score. These uninformed spectators miss what another teammate did to enable that player to sprint through toward the goal, and thus missed the true hero. That is, the player who decoyed a defender out of position, which in turn freed the player in possession of the ball to make his run to the goal or else they missed seeing the player that moved into the area near the player in possession of the ball. The teammate performed this maneuver to establish numerical superiority in the area of the ball. This player may have set up a wall pass that freed his teammate so that he could go on toward the goal. The awareness of support and establishing numerical superiority around the ball is crucial when learning and participating in passing, receiving, and controlling drills.

Is it important to pass merely to move a ball? Sometimes yes, because with each pass the defending team must adjust positions. The immediate scenario facing the team with the ball might not present a favorable stage for advancement of the ball. By merely passing off, you can wipe the slate clean and can start a new attack from a different position or angle. The new adjustment of the defense might present a weakness that the previous situation did not. If you move the ball, one of two things will happen, either the opponents move and make correct adjustments to accommodate the movement, or they will not move, move incorrectly, or move slowly. The more the ball moves, the more the opponents must make an accommodating adjustment. Thus the chance of an error on the part of the opponents increases.

In the first part of this chapter, there is a section on balance drilling. The first four drills are concerned with developing balance in the attack, midfield, and defensive sections of the field. Balance training helps individual players to develop their kinesthetic senses. However, the major emphasis of these four balance drills is passing, receiving, and controlling, while at the same time familiarizing players with their relative positions on the field.

Frequently we hear a coach yell "Don't Bunch" or "Spread Out". The coach is really asking that his team maintain both depth and width, which will create a balanced distribution of players on the field. This positioning enables the team to cover all sections of the field effectively. Width refers to coverage from side to side while depth refers to coverage from front to back, as seen in the following diagram.

SYMBOLS

Ⓐ **PLAYERS**

▼ **DEFENSE PLAYERS**

Ⓖ **GOALKEEPER**

Ⓢ **START OF BALL (IN DRILL)**

❶ **ORDER OF PASSES (IN DRILL)**

● **SUPPLY OF BALLS (NEEDED IN DRILL)**

→ → → **DIRECTION OF THE BALL**

⟶ **DIRECTION OF THE PLAYER**

〜〜〜⟶ **DRIBBLING**

⇥ ⇥ ⇥ **SHOT ON GOAL**

⚑ ⚑ **FLAG OR CONE** (Use one or the other when cone or flag is indicated.)

Drill 1-1

Obviously, it isn't humanly possible for a team to effectively cover the entire field and still maintain depth and width, we really mean coverage for a specific one-third of the field, the defensive area, the midfield area, and the attack area, as seen in the following diagram.

Drill 1-2

In each of these three sections of the field, it is possible to drill players to maintain balance. The following four drills can be used to accomplish this purpose.

Drill 1-3 Balance Training Drill 1

No. of players—Full team of 11 players

Explanation—Players line up in the attack section of the field as shown in the diagram below. You can use any system of play in

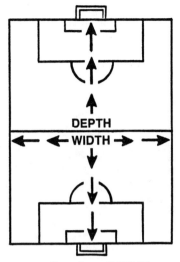

1-1 Depth and Width

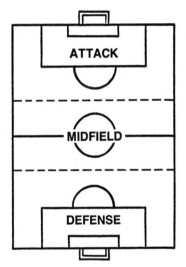

1-2 Defense, Mid-field, Attack

performing this drill—4-3-3, 4-2-4, etc. In this diagram a 4-2-4 system is used as an example.

In each of the three sections of the field, players can spend a portion of a practice session passing among themselves while maintaining positions that provide for depth and width. In the diagram

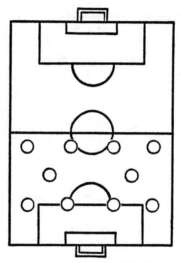

1-3 4-2-4 System of Play

you can see players arranged in the attack area of the field in a 4-2-4 system or arrangement. In this drill, players should maintain their relative positions.

Purpose—Players practice passing, receiving, and controlling while at the same time develop a kinesthetic sense of their positions in relation to the positions of their teammates.

Variation—When players can effectively pass one ball among themselves, then let them add a second ball, and as progress improves, a third and, finally, a fourth. By adding the extra balls more players are able to participate in the action of the drill. Instruct players to pass on the ground and only to those players who do not have a ball in their possession, are not in the act of receiving a ball, or are not in the act of passing a ball. This drill forces players to look around and make positive choices before they pass the ball. Emphasize to your players that they should look for possible places to pass the ball while the ball is approaching them. A player receiving a ball should move toward the ball as it approaches him. This drill is most effective when players use "1-touch" passing.

Drill 1-4 Balance Training—Drill II (No Diagram)

No. of players—Full team of eleven players plus four opponents

Explanation—When players master Balance Training (Drill I Four balls being passes at the same time) it is time to introduce opponents into the drill. Drill II is carried out in the same manner as Drill I except that defenders are introduced to oppose the passing of the attacking team. Start Drill II with one defender on the field. After a few minutes of play, add another defender, then another, progressively increasing the number of opponents until the effectiveness of the attacking players diminishes.

Defenders are instructed to get possession of the ball or balls and kick them out of bounds. When a ball is kicked out of bounds, the coach throws a new ball to a player who does not have a ball in his possession. The play in progress should remain continuous.

As the purpose of this drill is to practice maintaining depth and width, do not use more than four or five opponents. More than that number in this drill makes it too difficult to pass the ball around and the objective of the drill is then defeated. Maintain the action at all times.

Purpose—Players practice passing, receiving, and controlling, while at the same time develop a kinesthetic sense of their positions in relation to the positions of their teammates and their opponents' positions.

Drill 1-5 Balance Drill III—Follow the Ball (No Diagram)

No. of players—A full team of eleven players plus four defenders

Explanation—Same drill as Drill I and Drill II, only this drill starts using one ball and no defenders. As the drill progresses, introduce defenders one at a time until you have a total of four defenders on the field.

Play starts at one of the rear center positions. When a player passes to another player, he runs and follows the ball, taking up the position vacated by the receiving player. The next passer follows the same procedure. Even though place changing occurs, the depth and width should be maintained. Start this drill first without opponents, then introduce opponents, one at a time, until you have a total of four defenders on the field.

Purpose—The purposes are the same as in Drill I and Drill II, although in this drill, players practice exchanging positions and still maintaining their balance.

Drill 1-6 Drill IV—Look for Open and Attack Space (No Diagram)

No. of players—A full team of eleven players plus three or four opponents

Explanation—Players assume the same positions as in Drills I, II, and III. The ball is passed among the players until the coach blows the whistle. At this time, one more pass is permitted. This pass should be made into the space that best exploits the defending group and enables a teammate to get a good shot at the goal. Shots are taken in a "1-touch" or a "2-touch" fashion. Players must not move toward the goal until a whistle is blown and the ball is passed into the space that is being exploited. This delay will keep the attacking players conscious of the offside rule.

Purpose—The purposes are the same as in Drills I thru III, only in this drill players develop a sense for recognizing and taking advantage of the open attack space when an opportunity arises.

Note: The preceding drills were suggested for the attack area of the field, but they can be set up for practice in the mid-field and in the defensive sections of the field. However, slightly different tactics apply to those areas. For instance, in the defensive area, emphasis should be on moving the ball forward and avoiding the middle of the field in front of the goal. Also players can practice passing back to the goalkeeper to begin a new attack.

In mid-field, sometimes known as the preparation area for the attack, emphasis is on keeping possession of the ball and preparing for movement into the attack area of the field. Early in the season these drills can be used as a development tool and as the season progresses and as a specific need becomes evident these drills can be used for remedial purposes.

Drill 1-7 Quick Foot (No Diagram)

No. of players—Two per drill group

Distance—A and B are one yard apart and are facing each other.

Equipment—One ball per two players.

Explanation—A and B attempt to get control of a ball. They turn it and try to get their backs to their opponents.

Purpose—Players practice trying to get quick control of a ball. Players practice gaining control of a ball in a dropped-ball situation.

Drill 1-8 Receive, Pass, Move

No. of players—Three per drill group

Distance—A to B—10 to 15 yards, B to C—10 to 15 yards.

Explanation—A passes to B, B passes to C, B then runs to the other side and receives a pass back from C. B sends this pass on to A and then moves to the other side to receive the next pass.

Purpose—All players practice passing and player B practices moving to the open space to receive the pass.

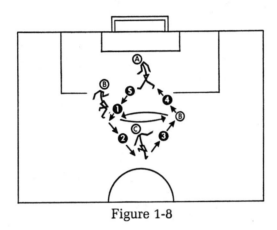

Figure 1-8

Drill 1-9 Place Changing

No. of players—Three per drill group

Distance—A to B—15 yards, A to C—15 yards, C to B—15 yards

Equipment—Three cones or flags

Explanation—A passes to B's place and C runs to receive the ball at B's place. Repeat. C returns the ball to A. C always receives the ball and B merely changes places each time. Rotate the position of A, B, and C after a period of time. Perform this drill at a slow pace when it is first introduced. As efficiency becomes evident, speed up the drill.

Purpose—Players practice passing, receiving, and place changing.

Variation—Using the same formation and the same drill, only A passes only to B's position and therefore players B and C alternate receiving and passing.

Figure 1-9

Drill 1-10 Pass, Turn, Pass

No. of players—Four per drill group

Distance—A to B—10 to 15 yards, B to C—10 to 15 yards, D to A—10 to 15 yards

Explanation—Play starts with a ball at A's feet. A passes to B, B turns the ball and passes to C. A takes B's place. B gets behind C. C then passes to A and A turns the ball and passes to D and so forth.

Purpose—Players practice moving into the open space.

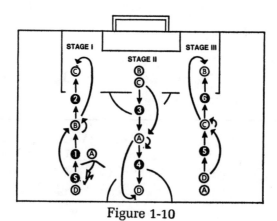

Figure 1-10

Drill 1-11 Three Man Wall Pass

No. of players—Four per drill group

Distance—The cones or flags form a thirty-yard square. As play improves, make the square smaller.

Equipment—Four cones or flags per drill group

Explanation—The defender must stay within the grid and he is instructed to play the ball. The defender tries to prevent the pass to B or C. If a pass is made to B, C immediately breaks to receive a second thru pass. Passes should be made on a "1-touch" basis. A should alternately fake a pass to one player and send it to the other.

Purpose—Players practice moving to the open space when they are not in possession of the ball.

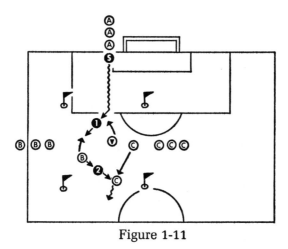

Figure 1-11

Drill 1-12 Pass and Trap Contest

No. of players—Four per drill group

Distance—The cones or flags are 10 to 15 yards apart

Equipment—Four cones or flags per group

Explanation—A passes on the ground to B, B passes to C etc. Each player must bring the ball to a complete stop before it is passed on. Groups compete to see which group can pass the ball around the cones a specified number of times in the shortest time possible. This contest is started on a signal (whistle).

Purpose—Players practice passing and trapping in a competitive environment.

Variation—The same procedure as above only players use a "1-touch" system to pass the ball around the cones or flags.

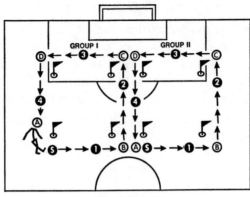

Figure 1-12

Drill 1-13 Star Passing

No. of players—Five per drill group

Explanation—A passes to B, B passes to C, C passes to D, etc.

Purpose—Players practice passing and receiving

Variation—The same drill only A passes to B and A replaces B. B passes to C and B replaces C, etc.

Variation—The same drill only use two balls. Start one ball at position A and the other ball at position C.

Figure 1-13

Drill 1-14 Long Pass and Overlap

No. of players—Five per drill group

Distances—Players form a forty- to fifty-yard square.

Explanation—A makes a long pass to player B. A overlaps and

takes B's position. B makes a long pass to C and takes up C's position, and so on. As soon as A makes the first pass and overlaps, E steps in and takes A's place.

Purpose—Players practice long passes. This drill is used to improve players organic fitness and is used to improve their long passing ability.

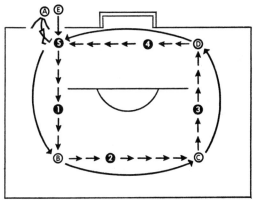

Figure 1-14

Drill 1-15 Pass and Follow

No. of players—Six per drill group

Distance—A to B—15 yards, B to C—15 yards

Explanation—F fills in for A in order to make the drill continuous after A passes and vacates his spot. A passes to B, A replaces B, F moves to occupy A's spot. B passes to C and B moves to replace C, C passes to A and C moves to replace A. A passes to D and A

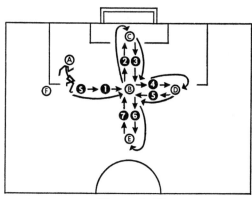

Figure 1-15

moves to replace D, D passes to C and D moves to replace C, C passes to E, etc.

Purpose—Players practice passing and receiving. They also practice switching positions and moving to the open space after making a pass.

Drill 1-16 Square and Go

No. of players—Six per drill group

Distance—A to B—20 yards.

Explanation—A passes to B, B makes a "1-touch" square pass back to A. B runs around the other B players waiting in line to receive a pass. B shoots at the goal. A goes to the back of B's line and B goes to the back of A's line. The diagram shows two groups executing the same drill.

Purpose—Players practice passing and then moving to open space for a return pass.

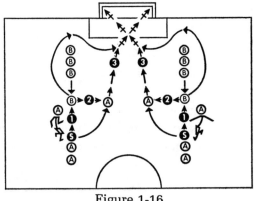

Figure 1-16

Drill 1-17 Adjusting to Legal Charge

No. of players—Six per drill group

Distance—A to D—20 yards, C to E—20 yards, A to B—10 yards

Equipment—Four soccer balls.

Explanation—A, C, D, and E have a ball at their feet. In turn, A, C, D, and E pass to B. The defender does not try to get the ball, but rather he bumps or nudges B when he is about to receive a ball. The defender must keep his actions (nudges) within the rules of a legal charge. After a period of time, players rotate positions.

Purpose—Players practice passing and receiving under close pressure from a defender. Player B practices coping and adjusting his body against a legal charge.

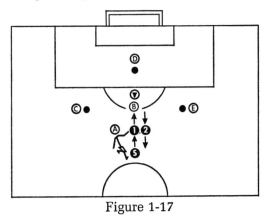

Figure 1-17

Drill 1-18 Two Groups Crossing

No. of players—Six per drill group

Distance—A to B—10 to 15 yards apart

Equipment—Two soccer balls

Explanation—Player A passes to player B. A gets in the end of B's line. B passes to C and B gets in the back of C's line. The second group A, B, and C repeat the same procedure simultaneously.

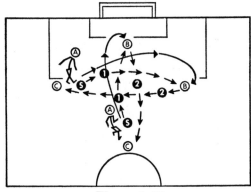

Figure 1-18

Purpose—Players practice passing, trapping and overlapping, to learn to maneuver in crowded areas, and because of this drill's strenuous nature your players' physical fitness will improve.

Drill 1-19 One on One Plus Wall Passers

No. of players—Six per drill group

Explanation—The defender and player A play one on one within the confines of the cones. A can use any B player to wall pass. If the defender wins the ball he continues in A's role by trying to make wall passes and receiving return passes. All B players are restricted to "1-touch" passes.

Purpose—Players practice wall passing.

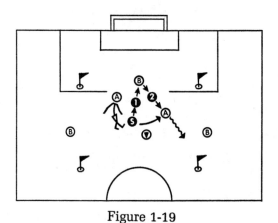

Figure 1-19

Drill 1-20 Eight Man Cross Passing

No. of players—Eight per drill group

Distance—A to B—15 to 20 yards, C to D—15 to 20 yards

Explanation—A kicks to B, and C kicks to D. After kicking all players move to the left and get behind the last player in that line. Now B passes to E while D passes to G. B runs to his left and gets behind G and D runs to his left and gets behind F.

Purpose—Two groups of players practice a passing drill that requires them to keep their heads up and concentrate on the next move.

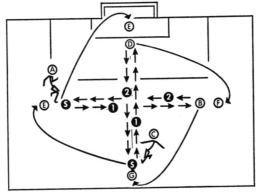

Figure 1-20

Drill 1-21 "1-touch" Four Ball Passing

No. of players—Six per drill group

Distance—B to D—20 yards, C to E—20 yards

Equipment—Four soccer balls.

Explanation—A runs around inside the square formed by B, C, D, and E, calling for and calling off passes. The defender tries to intercept the ball. A uses "1-touch" passing back to the player that passes the ball to him. A uses feints and changes of direction to get free to receive a pass.

Purpose—Players practice feints and fakes to get clear for passes.

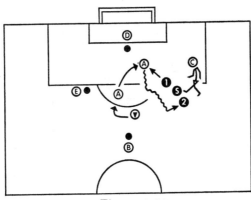

Figure 1-21

Drill 1-22 Pass or Dribble By

No. of players—Eleven or more

Equipment—Four grids are set up the length of the field. Each grid is approximately twenty yards by twenty yards.

Explanation—A tries to move a ball the length of the field with the help of player B. A progresses through each grid, one at a time. B and the defender must stay within their assigned grids. The defender tries to keep A from moving to the next grid. A and the defender are required to stay at the far end of the grid until A enters the front of the grid. A can dribble on to the next grid or use a wall pass and other passes with player B in order to beat the defender and to move on. It is played like two-on-one game. B should attempt to get clear of the defender and make it difficult for

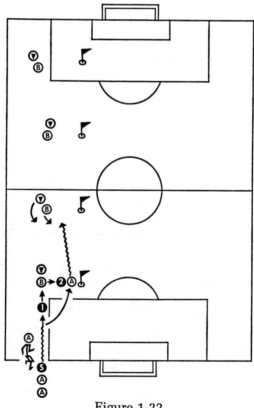

Figure 1-22

the defender to do his job. After breaking through the last grid, A tries to get a quick shot at the goal.

Purpose—A practices working in a two-on-one numerical advantage situation. B practices moving to a position to receive a pass and also moving to a position to sidetrack the defender. The defender practices breaking up or containing a two-on-one disadvantage situation.

Drill 1-23 Step on It and Go

No. of players—Twelve or more

Distance—A to B—25 yards, B to C—25 yards

Explanation—The second A in line passes the ball forward to the first A in line. A gathers the ball and passes to the first B. A gets in back of B's line. The first B receives the ball, steps on the ball, and makes a loop run toward C, and the second B in line sends a pass to the first B, etc.

Purpose—Players practice settling a ball and moving off to the open space for a pass.

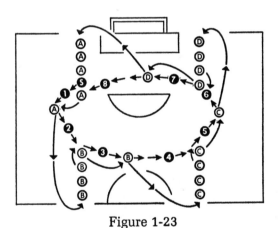

Figure 1-23

Drill 1-24 Square, Back, Thru

No. of players—Seven per drill group

Distance—Three groups of two players set up in the manner seen in the diagram.

Equipment—A supply of soccer balls.

Explanation—Play is started when the goalkeeper rolls or throws a ball to player A. A runs to meet the ball and passes it square to player B, while A runs behind B to receive a back pass from B. B runs forward to receive a through pass from A. B sends a long pass to C. C and D of Group II repeat the same procedure. After Group II completes this procedure the ball is sent to Group III for the same procedure. As a finale, F shoots at the goal. The goalkeeper throws another ball to A and the drill begins again.

Purpose—Players practice passing, receiving, and controlling long, medium length, and short passes as they move the ball up the field.

Variation—Other patterns of passing can be used for this drill. For example: Thru, Square, Back, Thru.

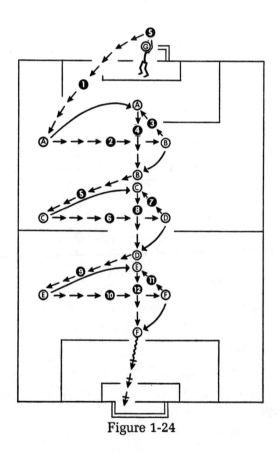

Figure 1-24

Drill 1-25 Table or Bench Wall Passing

No. of players—Any number

Distance—See the diagram

Explanation—A dribbles to the first cone and wall passes, then on to the next cone and repeats the same procedure.

Purpose—Players practice wall passing while moving up the field.

Variation—Instead of using benches to make wall passes, use players.

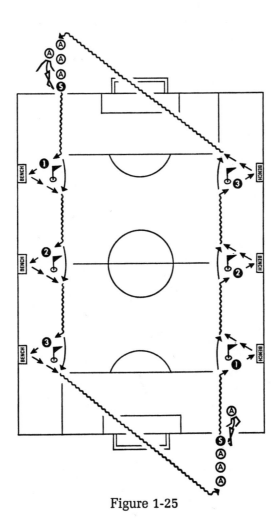

Figure 1-25

Drill 1-26 Collecting and Moving Off

No. of players—Unlimited

Distance—Players are placed around the perimeter of the center circle. A cone is placed in the center of the center circle. Four other cones are placed evenly ten yards outside the perimeter of the center circle. See the diagram.

Equipment—Five cones and one ball per player.

Explanation—The coach assigns each cone a number. Each player holds his ball at arm's length over his head. The coach yells out a specific trap and the number of one of the cones. Each player then releases his ball, performs the trap, and quickly moves toward the designated cone to touch it with his ball. After touching the cone with the ball, he dribbles back to his starting position.

Example—The coach yells out "Sole of the foot, Cone Three," and then blows a whistle for play to commense.

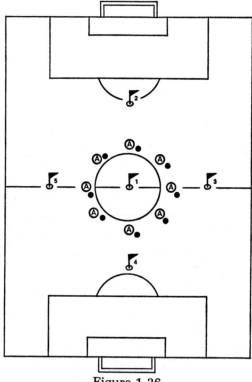

Figure 1-26

Purpose—Players practice quick control techniques in a competive atmosphere.

Drill 1-27 Six-Man Keep Away

No. of players—Eight per drill group

Distance—A to B—10 yards, B to C—10 yards, etc.

Explanation—Players A thru F pass around and across the circle. The defenders attempt to get possession of the ball. The player making a bad pass or causing the ball to be intercepted changes places with one of the defenders in the middle of the circle and play resumes.

Purpose—Players practice passing and receiving while being pressured by defenders.

Variation—The same drill only play "2-touch" or play "1-touch".

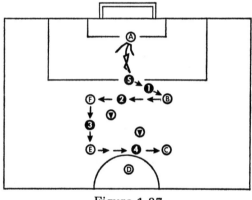

Figure 1-27

Drill 1-28 Up, Back, Thru

No. of players—Three per drill group

Distance—A to B—10 to 15 yards, B to C—10 to 15 yards

Explanation—A passes diagonally to B, B passes diagonally back to the open space and A moves to the space, controls the ball, and passes to C. C then repeats the same procedure.

Purpose—Players practice a basic passing combination—Up, Back, and Thru—and moving to the open space to receive a ball.

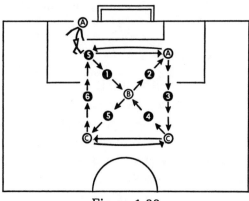

Figure 1-28

Drill 1-29 Chip on the Move

No. of players—Three per drill group

Distance—A to B—15 to 20 yards, B to C—30 yards apart

Explanation—While moving slowly down the field, A passes to B, B chips over A's head on a "1-touch" basis to C, and then C push-passes on the ground to A. A "1-touches" it back to C, C chips over A's head to B, and so on down the field. When players reach the other end of the field, they change places and come up the other side of the field performing the same pattern. Rotation order: A to B, B to C, C to A.

Purpose—Players practice passing and chipping while moving up the field.

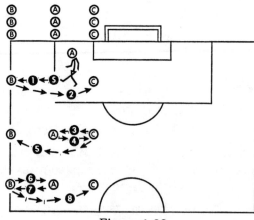

Figure 1-29

Variation—The same drill only the three players are arranged forward and back instead of alongside each other.

Drill 1-30 Two-on-One—"1-touch" (No Diagram)

No. of players—Three per drill group. Start three or four at one time.

Equipment—One ball per drill group

Explanation—Two players using a "1-touch" system inside the penalty area attempt to move a ball against a defender. If the defender gains control of the ball, the player making the mistake takes the defender's position. Players are restricted to playing the ball assigned to their group.

Drill 1-31 Move In

No. of players—Four per drill group

Distance—Place the cones fifteen yards apart.

Equipment—Four cones.

Explanation—A passes to the spot where B is located, D runs to B's spot to receive the ball while B takes D's place. D passes to C's spot and A and C change positions. A receives D's pass. Each time a pass is made players change places to receive the ball. First and third passes are diagonal and the second and fourth passes are straight forward.

Purpose—Players practice passing and receiving a ball, moving to the open space to receive a ball, and filling in the space that is vacated.

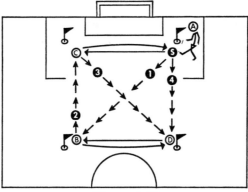

Figure 1-31

Drill 1-32 Move to the Ball

No. of players—Four per drill group

Distance—Cones or flags—5 yards apart, A to C—25 yards

Explanation—A and C have a ball at their feet. The defender attempts to stop passes from A or C to B. B runs around the cone or flag to receive a pass from A. B passes back to A. B can start to run to C and quickly turn back to A for another pass. The idea is for B to use his feints and change of pace runs to get clear for a pass from A or C.

Purpose—Player B develops the habit of running toward the ball and also develops his feinting and change of pace runs.

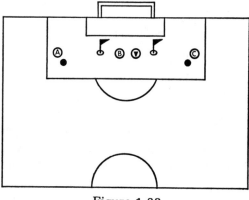

Figure 1-32

2

Heading

In attack and in defense, the technique of heading is a special skill that is necessary for an individual to master in order to become a complete soccer player. Some have it and some don't. Those that do have this ability add an extra dimension to their teams versatility.

In attack, heading is used to score goals, keep control of the ball, and pass the ball. In defense, players need heading skills for the same reasons as in attacking, but they also need heading ability to clear balls out of the immediate area surrounding the goal.

Sometimes, because of tight marking from the opponents, a player will head a ball rather than bring it to his feet. He heads a ball into open space and chases it, thus keeping control, or he heads it to a teammate and his team continues to keep control.

The modern four-back, compact defensive systems make it difficult to work the ball on the ground through the defense. Therefore, attackers must go down the wing and go to the air to penetrate the defense. You can see an important need for heading ability both in attack and in defense. Players are called on to head a ball in practically every direction during a game. Players head it forward, backward, sideways, while diving, leaping, and so forth. For these reasons, a variety of heading drills should be included in practice sessions to prepare players for match play.

Psychologists tell us that individuals tend to shy away from things that have produced frequent failure and fear. Many players are reluctant to head a ball because of injury or previous failures. Often, in a practice session, players can be shown how to improve their timing and learn to head the ball without injuring themselves.

The solution for improving a player's heading skills may be as simple as keeping his eyes on the ball longer, or the solution may be as complex as overcoming fear or an injury. Whichever is the case, patience, understanding, reassurance, and frequent drill sessions cannot hurt.

A variety of heading drills that reproduce activity found in match play sometimes can help your players to overcome these obstacles.

Heading drills can also be found in other chapters in this book. As heading can be considered a pass and also considered a shot on goal, some heading drills were included in the passing chapter and some in the shooting chapter and some even in the defensive chapter.

Drill 2-1 Wall Heading (No Diagram)

No. of players—One per drill

Explanation—The performer starts heading standing three feet away from a wall. He heads the ball repeatedly at the wall. After the performer becomes proficient at heading close to the wall, he should move further away from the wall and repeat the same procedure.

Purpose—Players practice controlled heading.

Drill 2-2 Rebound Heading

No. of players—Two per drill group

Explanation—A bounces the ball near the goal area and within B's reach. B tries to head the ball into the goal.

Purpose—Player B practices close in heading in this reaction drill.

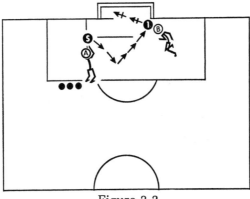

Figure 2-2

Drill 2-3 Dive Heading

No. of players—Two or more per drill group.

Stage I—Starting in a push-up position, B heads balls back to A. A throws the ball from a distance of five yards away from B. A throws the balls so that B must lunge in order to head the ball. B uses his hands to catch himself after heading the ball. A repeats the same procedure with players C, D, and E.

Stage II—The same drill as in Stage I, only the receiving player starts in a squatting position.

Stage III—The same drill as in Stages I and II, only the receiving player starts in a standing position.

Purpose—Players practice dive heading from three positions.

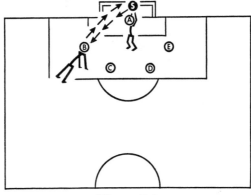

Figure 2-3

Drill 2-4 Circle and Head (No Diagram)

No. of players—Two per drill group

Distance—A to B—5 yards

Explanation—A throws balls toward B for B to head back to A. B moves in a circle around A while heading back to A. Periodically, A makes B jump to head the ball.

Variation—The same drill as above, only A walks down the field while B circles and heads back to A.

Drill 2-5 React and Head

No. of players—Three per drill group

Distance—Cones or flags form a ten-yard square

Explanation—C and B face away from the center of the square outlined by the cones or flags. B and C are outside the square and are opposite each other. A throws a ball high in the air between B and C and yells "BALL," B and C immediately turn and try to beat each other to the ball and head it over the line assigned to them before play begins.

Purpose—Players participate in a reaction drill used to improve their quickness.

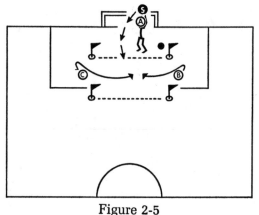

Figure 2-5

Drill 2-6 Wall Heading

No. of players–Three per drill group

Explanation—A throws the ball to B's head. B heads the ball square and high back to A. A runs to the ball and heads it at the goal.

Purpose—Players practice heading and head shooting.

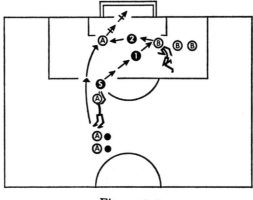

Figure 2-6

Drill 2-7 1 on 1 Heading

No. of players—Three per drill group

Explanation—A throws balls for B to head at the goal. B uses feints and change of pace runs to get away from the defender. B heads the ball at the goal. He then gets in the back of A's line.

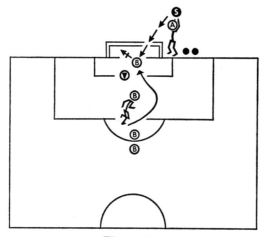

Figure 2-7

Purpose—Player B practices shooting at the goal with his head against a defender. B practices feints and change of pace runs in order to get free for a shot at the goal.

Drill 2-8 Head Left then Right

No. of players—Four per drill group

Distance—B to D—10 yards, B to C—10 yards, A to B—5 yards.

Explanation—A serves two balls toward B's head. B heads the first ball to his left to player D, and the second ball to player C on his right side.

Purpose—Player B practices heading balls to the right and to the left.

Figure 2-8

Drill 2-9 Heading Concentration

No. of players—Four per drill group

Explanation—On a signal (whistle), both A players throw a ball fifteen feet in the air toward the penalty shot line. The first B in each line tries to head the ball diagonally across from him.

Purpose—Player B practices heading in a congested area.

Drill 2-10 Head and Around the Cone

No. of players—Four per drill group

Distance—A cone or flag is placed on the center of the goal area line as seen in the diagram.

Explanation—A throws the ball in the air and B runs toward it and heads it at the goal. Then B runs around the cone or flag and repeats the same procedure with player C. A and C each have five balls to throw. A and C should keep B on the move.

Purpose—This is a pressure head shooting drill.

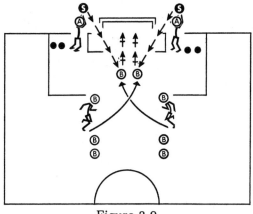

Figure 2-9

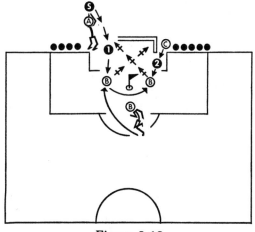

Figure 2-10

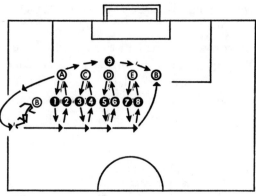

Figure 2-11

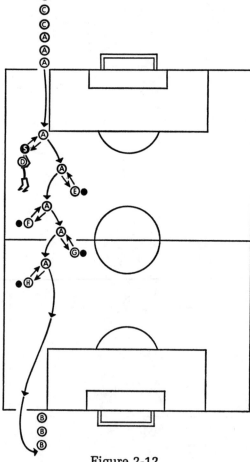

Figure 2-12

Drill 2-11 Line Heading

No. of players—Six per drill group

Explanation—A, C, D, and E each have a ball. In order, A, C, D, and E throw balls for B to head back to them. When B gets to the end of the line he runs behind the line of players and receives A's ball. A then starts down the line in the same manner as did B.

Purpose—Players practice heading while moving down the field.

Drill 2-12 Continuous Heading

No. of players—Fourteen per drill

Explanation—The first A runs toward D and D throws the ball toward A. A heads the ball back to D. A moves down the field and repeats the same procedure with E, F, G, and H. When all three As have completed the stint, Bs start up the field in the same fashion. When all Bs finish the stint, Cs start up the field. Play is continuous.

Purpose—This is a combination conditioning and heading technique practice drill.

Drill 2-13 Field Head Soccer (No Diagram)

No. of players—Twelve—six on six

Explanation—A regular game of soccer is played on one-half of the field. Goals are placed at the far ends of the field. The ball can be passed with the hands. After catching a ball, a player is permitted three steps before he must throw the ball. Players can only score by heading the ball into the goal.

Purpose—Players practice in a game designed to improve heading at the goal.

3

Dribbling, Feinting, Screening, Rhythm Changes, and Dribbling Tricks

Dribbling—The ball is controlled by the performer and it is moved on the ground. The ball should be kept close to the performer.

Feinting—Feinting is moving your body in a way that will make an opponent think you are going in one direction when you are in fact going in another.

Screening—These are movements of the body used to protect the ball from an opponent by using the body to shield the ball.

Rhythm Changes—These are change-of-pace movements used to lull an opponent into a false sense of security.

Dribbling Tricks—These movements involve a combination of rhythm changes, screening techniques, feinting skills, and dribbling moves used to protect and control a ball.

Each of the above movements has a separate purpose. Yet, when used in a game by a skilled performer, they appear as one skill. The more these skills become instinctive reactions, the more valuable and effective they become to the player.

The above defined skills are especially valuable for all players when they are in the immediate vicinity of the goal. These skills enable an attacker to confuse, disrupt, and create numercial superiority and scoring opportunities. In mid-field and in the defending areas of the field, limited dribbling is sometimes used when passing lanes are closed. They are also used when it is necessary to bide time and keep possession of the ball until further opportunities appear for a pass.

Each of the skills are taught separately, and then are combined and practiced on an individual basis. Once players can exhibit a reasonable performance level, it is time to practice the skills with other players. This type of drill can be performed inside a grid. Players can dribble, feint, screen, and make change-of-pace runs inside a grid. The size of the grid depends on the number of participants. For example, ten players can use a grid ten yards by ten yards. For more players, you can increase the size of the grid. In a ten-by-ten yard grid players can dribble in and out of the other players trying to avoid touching another player's ball. On a whistle, players can practice screening their balls from the other players in the grid, when a whistle blows two times, players can make change-of-pace runs.

This chapter contains a variety of tricks, feints, change-of-pace techniques, and a combination of these techniques. Once players have been exposed to the various possibilities suggested to them, they should be encouraged to refine and to develop their own. Remember that it is better to know a few of these techniques well, rather than knowing many of them only half way.

Once a player has perfected these skills, he should practice them against an opponent. Going one-on-one inside a ten-by-ten-yard grid will develop these skills further. Other one-on-one drills are found in this chapter and also in the chapter on defense and tackling.

Further perfecting and gaining experience at dribbling, feinting, screening, and rhythm changes can be performed in small-sided games and in scrimmages. In inter-squad scrimmages and small group games, an individual can experiment and find out what works best for him.

Players should practice basic dribbling skills until these skills are automatic. Once these skills are mastered, they can progress to more complex methods of feinting and dribbling tricks. This requires experimenting on his own and practice, practice, practice. If a player practices fifteen minutes a day on his own for one year his dribbling, feinting, and screening skills will enable him to beat many opponents.

The idea behind any feint or fake is to cause an opponent to make a bad move and then to capitilize on his mistake. When taking on an opponent, the performer should make a move, wait for the opponent to react to this movement, and then quickly accelerate past the opponent.

Sometimes a player can use a supporting player to help him disguise his intentions. He does this by making it appear as if he will pass off to the supporting player, and then keeping the ball and dribbling past the opponent.

Often a dribbler can apply pressure to an opponent, then back off. When the opponent relaxes, the dribbler then accelerates past the opponent. Frequently, after pressure is applied and quickly removed, the defending player will react by relaxing. A good dribbler is like a good magician. Both lull people into thinking and expecting one thing, when their initial actions are used to disguise what will really happen.

Inviting and teasing an opponent to react to play a ball at the wrong time is a technique used by some dribblers to force an opponent to make a bad move. When the opponent reaches for the ball, the dribbler pulls it back, pushes it past the opponent, and dribbles on toward the goal.

The physical qualities that can be developed to make an effective dribbler include speed, balance, flexibility, agility, reaction time, peripheral vision, and a kinesthetic sense. Individuals are born with a certain potential in each of these areas, but rarely do they reach this potential. This happens because not enough time is dedicated to developing these areas of preparation. A coach should encourage his players to spend more time and energy to develop these individuals skills. Further, he can suggest specific moves for individual players to practice on their own.

The mental qualities necessary to be an effective dribbler include confidence, courage, persistance, and the ability to analyze one's own personal abilities and personal shortcomings. A coach, to a limited extent, can help his players to develop confidence, courage, and persistence through his encouragement. A coach can also help a player to improve his understanding of his personal abilities and personal shortcomings by his critical comments and his verbal encouragement. In the final analysis, however, the extent that these mental qualities will improve is up to the individual.

Drill 3-1 Basic Dribbling Practice Exercises (No Diagram)

No. of players—One per drill

Explanation—While traveling down the length of the field players perform the following exercises:

1. Using the inside of the foot to dribble
2. Using the instep to dribble
3. Using the outside of the foot to dribble
4. Each individual performs the above dribbling methods in small circles.
5. The same as the preceding drill only players dribble a ball in a figure eight pattern.

Drill 3-2 Basic Dribbling Practice Using Cones or Flags (NO Diagram)

No. of players—One per drill

Explanation—Set up ten cones in a row, four or five yards separating each cone.

1. Players dribble down the left side of the cones using the outside of the left foot.
2. Players dribble down the right side of the cones using the outside of the right foot.
3. Players dribble in and out of the cones while dribbling with the outside of the foot. When passing each cone the dribbler should dribble with the furthest foot away from the cone. For example, in passing a cone on his right, he should use the outside of his left foot. While passing a cone on his left, he should use the outside of his right foot.

Drill 3-3 Dribbling and Tricks (No Diagram)

No. of players—One per drill

Equipment—One ball for each player

Explanation—Players dribble a ball the entire length of the field performing feints and tricks. Before each trip, the coach designates the feint or trick he wants his players to perform. While they are dribbling, the coach blows the whistle to let the players know when he wants them to perform the assigned trick or feint. The following are just a few of the many tricks and feints a coach can use.

1. Dribble, fake a short pass, and dribble.

2. Dribble, fake a long pass, and dribble.

3. Dribble, perform head and shoulder feints, and dribble.

4. Dribble, stop the ball with the sole of the foot. Pull it behind, screen it, and turn and dribble.

5. Dribble, stop the ball with the sole of the foot. Pull it behind and screen it. Shoulder and body fake going one way, turn it and go the other way.

6. Dribble, stop the ball with the sole of the foot, then push it forward with the sole of the foot and continue in the same direction.

7. Dribble, stop the ball, fake pushing or passing the ball with the inside of the right foot. Pass your foot over the ball, feint to left, and push the ball to the right with the outside of the right foot.

8. Dribble, stop the ball with the sole of the foot, pull the ball behind you and across the back of the supporting foot. Shift your weight off the supporting foot to the other foot and push the ball forward with the nonsupporting foot.

9. Dribble, swerve you body to the right, then straighten up and take the ball to your left with the inside of the right foot.

10. Dribble, fake pushing the ball with the outside of the right foot, pass your foot over the ball, and take it to the left with the inside of the right foot.

11. Dribble, lift the right foot over the ball and place it on the left side of the ball, shift your weight to the right foot and play the ball to the left with the inside of the left foot.

12. Dribble, fake stopping it with the sole of the foot, bring the foot behind the ball, and push it forward with the instep, and dribble.

13. Dribble slowly, then sprint forward in a diagonal direction for five yards, then dribble slowly for five yards and repeat the same procedure.

14. Dribble, when the whistle blows players perform feints and tricks of their own choosing.

Purpose—Players practice dribbling, feinting, and screening.

Drill 3-4 Dribble, Pass, Turn, and Dribble

No. of players—Two per drill group

Distance—A to B—30 yards

Explanation—A and B, on signal, dribble toward each other. When they get within ten yards of each other, they pass their balls straight ahead slowly. A retrieves B's ball and B retrieves A's ball. Both players dribble back to their original starting positions.

Purpose—Players practice dribbling, passing skills, and controlling skills.

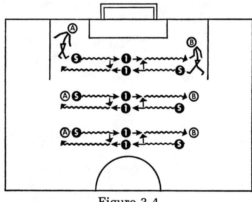

Figure 3-4

Drill 3-5 Dribble, Pass, Receive.

No. of players—Three per drill group

Distance—B to C—30 yards

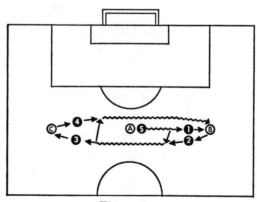

Figure 3-5

Explanation—A dribbles toward B. A passes off to B. B "1-touch" passes back to A. A then dribbles toward C and repeats the same procedure.

Purpose—Players practice dribbling, passing, and receiving.

Drill 3-6 Screening

No. of players—Three per drill group

Explanation—A throws a ball for B to collect and then to screen from the defender. For a period of five seconds, B screens the ball by keeping his back to the defender. B must stay inside the penalty area lines.

Purpose—Player B practices screening and protecting the ball from the defender.

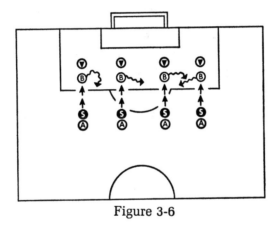

Figure 3-6

Drill 3-7 Feinting (No Diagram)

No. of players—One per drill

Equipment—One ball per player

Distance—A row of cones or flags (five or more) are set up. Each cone is ten yards away from the next cone.

Explanation—Each player dribbles toward each cone and performs a feint with his shoulders or knees and moves on to the next cone and performs the same procedure.

Purpose—Players practice dribbling and feinting.

Drill 3-8 Bench Drill

No. of players—One per drill

Equipment—Two benches

Distance—The two benches are placed twenty yards apart as seen in the diagram.

Explanation—A dribbles to the first bench and chips his ball over the bench. He then jumps over the bench and retrieves his ball, and then repeats the same procedure at the next bench. When over the second bench, he shoots at the goal.

Purpose—Players practice dribbling and shooting. This is an agility drill.

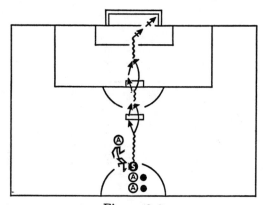

Figure 3-8

Drill 3-9 One-on-One

No. of players—Two per drill group

Explanation—Each A player has a ball and is assigned a defender. A players dribble inside the penalty area restraining lines, and defenders try to kick the ball out of the penalty area. When all A players are eliminated, players change roles. Defenders become As and As become defenders.

Purpose—Players practice offensive dribbling while defenders practice tackling skills.

Variation—The same drill only defenders are not included. A players try to protect their balls and at the same time try to kick the other A player's balls out of the penalty area.

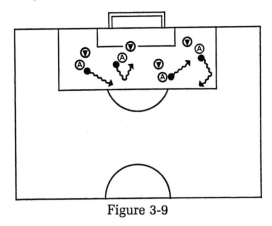

Figure 3-9

Drill 3-10 Take Over

No. of players—Two per drill group

Distance—A to B—5 yards

Explanation—A dribbles diagonally across and in front of B. When A passes by B, A leaves the ball and B picks it up and dribbles diagonally off a few yards. B then turns diagonally back and repeats the same procedure with player A. This procedure is repeated down the field.

Purpose—Players practice dribbling and take-over maneuvers.

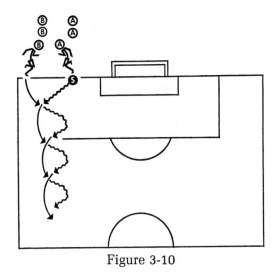

Figure 3-10

Drill 3-11 Dribble and Push Ahead (No Diagram)

No. of players—Two per drill group

Explanation—A dribbles a ball three yards ahead of B, A pushes the ball ahead of himself a few feet, B sprints from behind A to in front of A and continues to dribble a few feet. This procedure is repeated down the field.

Purpose—Players practice dribbling.

Drill 3-12 Dribble and Exchange

No. of players—Three per drill group

Distance—A to B—30 yards, A to C—one yard.

Explanation—A dribbles toward B, just before A gets to B, A steps on the ball and B picks it up and dribbles toward C, etc. Start play on the side where two players (C and A) are located.

Purpose—Players practice dribbling skills and improve their fitness.

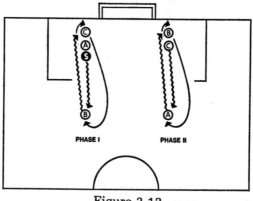

Figure 3-12

Drill 3-13 Dribble Around the Cone

No. of players—Three per drill group

Explanation—B runs toward A, A passes to B. B gathers the ball and dribbles around the cone and passes back to A. B then runs around the cone and receives a ball from C. Play continues until B has repeated this procedure ten times.

Purpose—B practices a combination skill of controlling and dribbling.

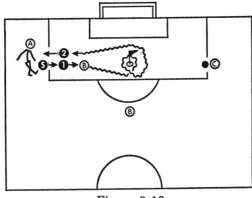

Figure 3-13

Drill 3-14 Escape

No. of players—Eight per drill group

Explanation—On a signal, the defenders sprint toward the goal. A players try to dribble a ball and to escape to the outside of the penalty area.

Purpose—A practices dribbling and feinting against an opponent.

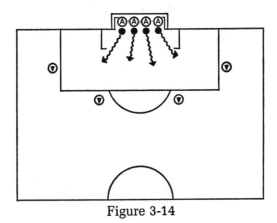

Figure 3-14

Drill 3-15 Beat the Defender

No. of players—Eight per drill group

Equipment—Two goals—A twenty-five-yard field.

Explanation—Play is continuous. Players line up as seen in the diagram. Each A player has a ball and attempts to score in his assigned goal. If a defensive player wins the ball, he tries to score in his assigned goal. If a ball goes out-of-bounds or over the end lines, play is started again by the opponent of the player who last touched the ball. When a score occurs, the ball is brought back to the center and started again by the player who did not score. Players attack and defend against their assigned opponents only.

Purpose—Players practice offensive dribbling skills. Players also practice defensive skills in a one-on-one situation in a congested area.

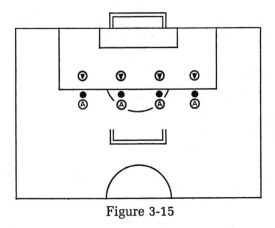

Figure 3-15

Drill 3-16 Traffic Dribbling

No. of players—Unlimited

Equipment—One ball per player, four cones.

Explanation—A thirty-yard square is marked off with four cones. All players start in the middle of the square. On a signal (whistle), players dribble around each cone in the order indicated in the diagram. Players are instructed not to let their balls touch other player's balls. To promote more interaction, make the square smaller.

Purpose—Players practice dribbling and controlling a ball in a highly congested area.

Variation—Select two teams of equal number of players. Teams compete to see which team can dribble around the cones in the shortest period of time. One team dribbles around the cones in the following order; 1, 2, 3, 4. Whereas the other team uses the opposite order—4, 3, 2, 1.

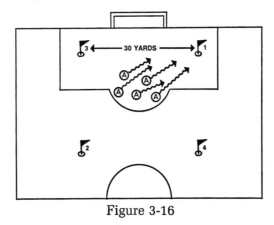

Figure 3-16

Drill 3-17 Rhythm Changes

No. of players—Unlimited

Equipment—Ten or more cones, one ball per player

Explanation—Cones can be set up in any arrangement. There should be five yards between cones. Players dribble slowly to the first cone and dribble 360 degrees around it. When the first player has dribbled around the first cone another players starts. After a player slowly dribbles around the first cone he sprints to the second cone and quickly dribbles 360 degrees around it, etc. After dribbling around each cone players change the pace of their runs.

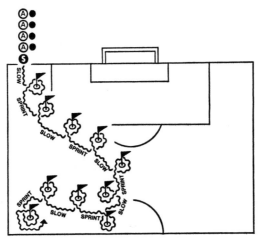

Figure 3-17

When each player reaches the last cone, he immediately dribbles back against traffic in the same manner—slow, sprint, etc.

Purpose—Players practice dribbling in a congested setting and practice change-of-pace runs.

Drill 3-18 Circle and Take Over

No. of players—Two per drill group

Explanation—A dribbles around the circle. B runs around the circle in the other direction. Half-way around the circle, A leaves the ball, B picks it up and dribbles around the circle. A runs around the circle and repeats the same procedure.

Purpose—Players practice dribbling and take over maneuvers.

Variation—Each player has a ball and the players exchange balls half way around the circle.

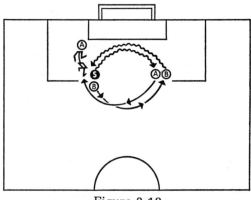

Figure 3-18

Drill 3-19 Two on One Dribble

No. of players—Four per drill group

Explanation—A attempts to beat the two defenders by using his dribbling skill.

Purpose—Player A practices dribbling in a two-against-one situation.

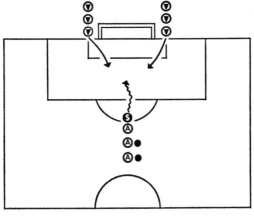

Figure 3-19

Drill 3-20 Circle Dribble

No. of players—Ten or more

Explanation—Players start out dribbling around the circle. On a signal, players dribble directly across the circle. They should dribble quickly and should avoid interfering with the other players.

Purpose—Players practice dribbling in a congested area.

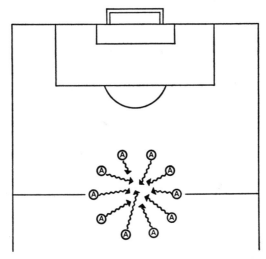

Figure 3-20

Drill 3-21 Dribble Ten Yards (No Diagram)

No. of players—Two teams of an equal number of players. If there are fewer than five players on each team use one-half of a soccer field, if there are more than five per team use the entire field.

Explanation—The game is played like a regular game of soccer only the player in possession of the ball is required to dribble ten yards before he passes the ball to another player. Passes are not permitted over ten yards.

Purpose—Players practice their dribbling skills.

4

Shooting

A team's ability to score more goals than its opponent usually determines the outcome of a game. Scoring ability and scoring potential take a long time to develop. Not only must a good scorer have many skills, but he must be able to execute these skills swiftly, positively, and confidently.

A major emphasis in shooting drills should be on accuracy. Accuracy depends largely on concentration on the correct execution of skills. Accuracy and concentration are a prerequisite to developing powerful shots. If power is emphasized before accuracy, it is like putting the cart before the horse. Therefore, when teaching shooting drills, a coach should at all times be stressing accuracy and let power take care of itself.

The outcome of any soccer game is determined by goals successfully scored, and opportunities to score in a game are infrequent. These two statements indicate that accurate shooting is paramount in the preparation of players for match play.

It is important to know where goals are scored and how far from the goal they are scored when setting up drills for shooting practice. We know that most goals are scored within the penalty area and that the closer we are to the goal the better our chances for success. We also know that the chance of scoring is greater in front of the goal rather than from the sides. But, how can this information be incorporated and used in setting up shooting drills? You will notice that most of the shooting drills in this book are designed so that the final release of the shot on goal is in front of the goal and inside the penalty area. Statistically, experts tell us that most goals are scored from these areas. When setting up your shooting drills, these factors should be a major consideration.

Opportunities to score disappear quickly, therefore "1-touch" shooting practice is a must. Balls approach from a variety of angles, at various speeds, and at various heights during a game. Through a variety of shooting drills, a player can sharpen his skills to meet the challenges that he will be facing in match play.

All field players on the team should participate in shooting drills. In today's game, where players are coming from the rear to score, there is a definite need for these rear players to participate and practice in the skill drills necessary for scoring goals. Rear players, that is mid-field players and defenders, should possess the skills of an attacking forward. They should be able to shoot with either foot, be able to recognize and use open space, and be able to shoot and keep a ball low to the ground. Furthermore, they should know how and when to make decoy runs and blind side runs, and to get clear for a shot on goal. They should also have a strong desire to score when an opportunity develops. All field players should be prepared to use skills that are necessary for the position to which they are assigned, as well as be able to take up an attack position or a defensive position when called on to do so.

In this chapter you will find a variety of shooting drills that relate to what happens in match play.

The last ten drills (4–25 to 4–34) in this chapter are shooting drills that incorporate a preliminary maneuver to free a player for a shot at the goal. Back passes, wall passes, loop runs, and so forth are used to free players for a shot at the goal. In a short period of time, all players can get multiple chances to participate in the maneuvers necessary to free a teammate for a shot at the goal. Further, and just as important, they get multiple chances to shoot at the goal.

Once players get to know the mechanics of these drills, a coach can accomplish much in a short period of time.

In order for these drills to run smoothly, at least three players are needed in each of the four starting positions.

Drill 4-1 Volley Shooting (No Diagram)

No. of players—One per drill

Explanation—Players stand just inside the eighteen-yard line and in front of the goal. Each player has a ball in his hands and is facing away from the goal. Each player throws his ball over his head, then turns, and volleys or half volleys his ball into the goal.

Purpose—Players practice volley and half-volley shooting.

Drill 4-2 Go Behind

No. of players—Two per drill group

Distance—A to B—10 to 15 yards

Explanation—A dribbles diagonally to his right. B cuts close behind A to receive a through pass. B shoots at the goal.

Variation—Introduce a defender to the drill. Whether or not A passes to B depends on the position of the defender.

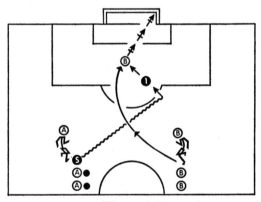

Figure 4-2

Drill 4-3 Turning and Shooting Combinations

No. of players—Two per drill group

Distance—A to B—5 yards, B to the goal—6 to 10 yards

Explanation—A serves balls to B. The coach, before each serve, designates the height at which the ball should be thrown. B's back is to the goal. Before each throw the coach instructs which combination he would like to see B perform. The coach can start with

"1-touch" shooting and progress with two and three juggling combinations before shooting.

Possible combinations: "1-touch"

1. "1-touch" shooting
2. Carry it or let it go through and shoot

Possible combinations: "2-touch"

1. Thigh, turn, and shoot—the ball is thrown in the air to B's thigh.
2. Head, turn, and shoot—the ball is thrown in the air to B's head.
3. Chest, turn, and shoot—the ball is thrown in the air to B's chest.
4. Pop the ball in the air to either side, turn, and shoot—the ball is thrown in the air toward B's feet.
5. Pick the ball up with the foot, turn, and shoot—the ball is rolled toward B's feet.

Possible combinations: "3-touch"

1. Thigh, foot, turn, and shoot—the ball is thrown in the air to B's thigh.
2. Chest, thigh, turn, and shoot—the ball is thrown in the air to B's chest.
3. Push it to the right with the right foot, pull it back to the left with the sole of the right foot, and shoot—the ball is rolled to B's feet.

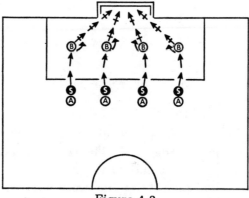

Figure 4-3

4. Let it go through, push it to the right with the outside of the right foot and shoot—balls are thrown at B's chest.

These are just a sample of the many combinations that are possible. This same drill can be performed against a net or indoors in the off-season.

Purpose—Players practice shooting and shooting preliminary skills.

Drill 4-4 Check In—Check Out

No. of players—Two per drill group

Distance—A to B—15 to 20 yards

Explanation—B checks back to receive a pass from A. B gives a "1-touch" short pass back to A. A dribbles outside of B's line while B breaks to the inside and receives a pass from A. B then shoots at the goal.

Rotation order—A to B.

Purpose—Players practice a basic combination used to get free for a shot at the goal.

Variation—Put a defender to guard B. If B is covered, A shoots.

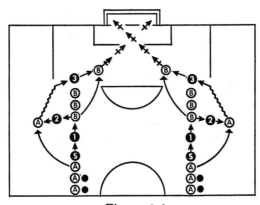

Figure 4-4

Drill 4-5 Juggle Inside the Penalty Area and Shoot (No Diagram)

No. of players—One per drill

Explanation—Players juggle a ball inside the penalty area until the coach blows a whistle. Immediately on hearing the whistle, players shoot at the goal.

Purpose—Players practice juggling and shooting skills.

Variation—Use the same drill but include opponents. Players start juggling the ball with their backs to the defender. When the whistle blows, each juggler tries to turn the ball and get a quick shot off at the goal.

Drill 4-6 Juggle and Shoot (No Diagram)

No. of players—One per drill

Equipment—One ball per player

Distance—Cones or flags are five yards away and in front of the penalty area line.

Explanation—A, B, C, and D juggle a ball from the cones or flags to the eighteen-yard line. As soon as they get near the eighteen-yard line, each vollies his ball into the goal. The ball should not touch the ground while the player is juggling.

Purpose—Players practice juggling and shooting at the goal.

Note: (Drills 4–5 and 4–6) When your players do not possess the ability to juggle, a coach can allow one bounce on the ground between juggles.

Drill 4-7 Agility Shooting

No. of players—Two per drill group

Distance—Cones are two yards apart. There are five yards between the last cone and the middle of the two flags. A tape or string is strung between the two flags. This tape or string is two feet high.

Explanation—Each A, one at a time, dribbles around the cones as seen in the diagram. After passing the last cone, A passes the ball under the string or tape. He jumps over the tape, runs to the ball, and "1-touches" it into the goal.

Purpose—This is an agility drill that includes dribbling and shooting.

Variation—The same drill only players dribble and shoot with the outside of the foot.

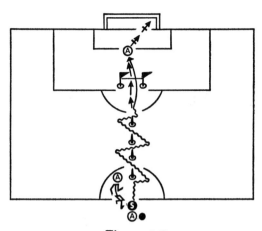

Figure 4-7

Drill 4-8 Gyro Shooting

No. of players—Two per drill group

Equipment—Five balls evenly spaced along the eighteen-yard line. See the diagram.

Explanation—Each player is timed for his performance. On a signal, the first A in line runs to the nearest ball to him and shoots it in the goal. A then turns 360 degrees and moves on to the next ball and so on. The time is stopped when he kicks the last ball at the goal.

Purpose—Players practice quick shooting after performing a disorienting stunt.

Variation—Players perform a forward roll after shooting each ball.

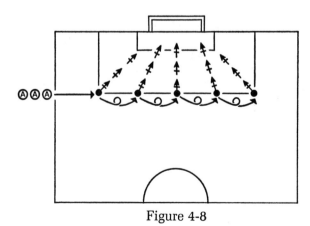

Figure 4-8

Drill 4-9 Reaction Shooting

No. of players—Three per drill group

Explanation—A has a supply of balls. B faces away from the goal. A throws balls behind B and yells "Ball!" B turns and attempts a "1-touch" shot at the goal.

Purpose—This is a reaction drill. Player B practices getting his shots off quickly.

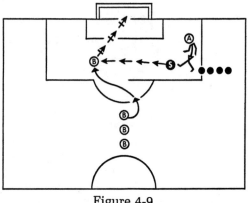

Figure 4-9

Drill 4-10 Shoot Out

No. of players—Three per drill group

Explanation—Balls are placed on the eighteen-yard line as seen in the diagram. On a signal, players A, B, and C shoot at the goal

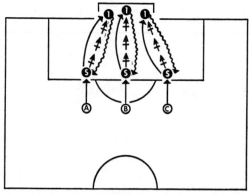

Figure 4-10

Then they sprint to recover the balls out of the net or goal. They dribble back to the eighteen-yard line and shoot again. This procedure is repeated five times. The first person finished is the winner. If a shooting player misses he must retrieve his ball, dribble it back in front of the goal, and shoot it again.

Purpose—Players practice accurate shooting. This drill is also used to improve speed and stamina.

Drill 4-11 Eighteen Corner and Cut

No. of players—Three per drill group

Explanation—On a signal (whistle), A dribbles along the base line and B runs to the corner of the eighteen-yard line and cuts toward the goal. A passes to B and B shoots at the goal with the inside of his foot. All shots are taken on a "1-touch" basis.

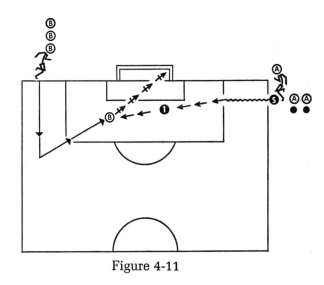

Figure 4-11

Drill 4-12 Away from the Goalkeeper

No. of players—Three per drill group

Explanation—A goalkeeper is continually walking across the inside of the goal. When he reaches the far post he walks back again, etc. Balls are rolled across the face of the goal from various angles by player A. B runs to the ball and shoots with the inside of his foot.

B is instructed to shoot at the open side of the goal. If the goalkeeper is on the right side B obviously should shoot to the left side.

Purpose—Players practice close-in accurate shooting.

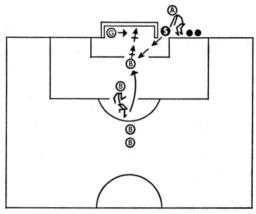

Figure 4-12

Drill 4-13 1, 2, Shooting

No. of players—Three per drill group

Explanation—A throws balls high in the air to the middle of the eighteen-yard line. B runs toward the ball, taps it with his foot or thigh, and volleys it into the goal.

Purpose—Players practice juggling on the run and volley shooting.

Variation—The same drill only shooting is done on a one-half volley fashion.

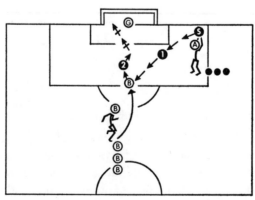

Figure 4-13

Drill 4-14 Shooting Timing

No. of players—Three per drill group

Explanation—A passes to B, B passes to C, C passes to A. A shoots at the goal. C retrieves the ball and gets in the back of B's line. B gets in the back of A's line and A gets in the back of C's line.

Purpose—This is a combination drill involving passing, receiving, and shooting. Players practice timing their run so they arrive at the right time to receive the ball on the run.

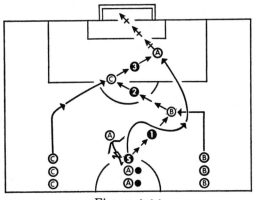

Figure 4-14

Drill 4-15 Turn It

No. of players—Three per drill group

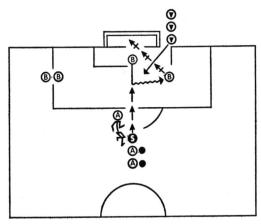

Figure 4-15

Explanation—A kicks a ball toward B. As soon as the ball is kicked a defender comes onto the field and tries to tackle B. B tries to get a shot on the goal.

Rotation order: A to B, B to the defender, the defender to A.

Purpose—Player B practices receiving, turning, feinting, and shooting.

Drill 4-16 One-on-One Either Goal

No. of players—Four per drill group

Equipment—Two cones or flags, a supply of balls.

Explanation—A serves a ball to B and C through the cones. B and C attempt to get control of the ball and to get a quick shot off at either of the small goals set up at the far ends of the eighteen area as seen in the diagram. Once B or C gets control of the ball, they should use feints and quick changes of direction to get free for a shot at either of the goals. The player who is not in possession of the ball tries to win the ball back and to attempt a shot at either goal.

Purpose—Players practice getting control of a ball and shooting quickly. They also practice dribbling and feinting skills in a one-on-one situation.

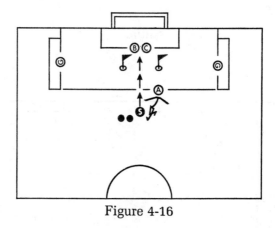

Figure 4-16

Drill 4-17 Ten Ball Shooting Pressure

No. of players—Four per drill group

Explanation—A passes across the penalty area, B sprints to the ball and "1-touches" it into the goal. B runs around the cone and receives the second ball from C, B shoots and runs back around the cone, etc. A and C each serve five balls. Balls are served in a manner that keeps player B running.

Purpose—Player B improves his physical fitness and at the same time improves his "1-touch" shooting skill. This is a pressure drill.

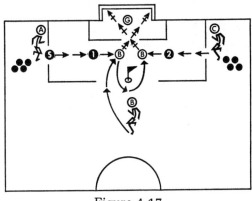

Figure 4-17

Drill 4-18 Lay It Off

No. of players—Three per drill group

Explanation—A passes forward to B, B lays the ball off for C to sprint in and take a shot at the goal.

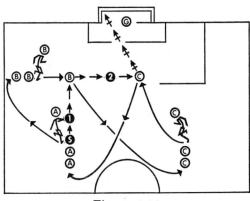

Figure 4-18

Rotation order: A to B, B to C, C to A.

Purpose—This is a timing drill. The idea is for C to time his run to arrive with speed. Shots at the goal are on a 1-touch basis.

Variation—Repeat the same drill, only start play from the other side of the field.

Drill 4-19 Cone Kick Down

No. of players—Four on four or five on five

Equipment—Ten cones

Distance—On half of a soccer field set up five cones at each end as seen in the diagram. There is a distance of two feet between cones.

Explanation—This game is played with goalkeepers. A team attempts to knock all five cones over with the ball before B team does the same to their assigned cones. When the ball goes over the endline, it is treated like a goalkick or a corner kick in a regular game. Balls going over the sidelines are thrown back into play.

Purpose—Players develop accurate shooting skill.

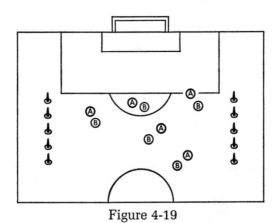

Figure 4-19

Drill 4-20 Follow Up

No. of players—Four per drill group

Distance—A to B—15 to 20 yards, B to C—15 to 20 yards.

Explanation—A passes to B, B wall passes back to A. A passes diagonally to his left and player C runs forward and shoots at the goal. A and B follow up C's shot with A moving to the edge of the goal area in front of the far post and B moving to the edge of the goal area in front of the near post. All shots should be placed rather than blasted.

Purpose—Players practice a three-man combination used to free a player for a shot at the goal. Players practice timing their runs.

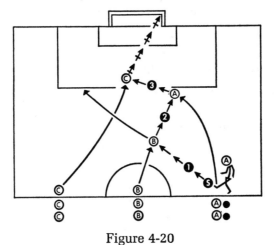

Figure 4-20

Drill 4-21 Four-on-Two Counterattack

No. of players—Seven per drill group

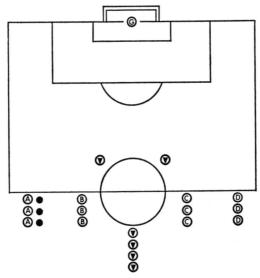

Figure 4-21

Explanation—Play starts at player A's position. A, B, C, and D start a quick counterattack against two defenders. Players are instructed to move quickly toward the goal.

Purpose—A, B, C, and D practice a quick counterattack against two defenders. Players practice using their numerical superiority.

Variation—The same drill only play starts at B, C, or D position.

Drill 4-22 Shoot or Return

No. of players—Seven per drill group

Explanation—One at a time B, C, D, E, and F feed balls to player A. Balls are served one at a time in rapid succession. Some are served on the ground and others should be chipped in the air. A tries to get the shot off quickly and prepare himself for the next shot. If he is not ready for a shot, A can pass back to the player who passed to him.

Purpose—Player A practices choosing quickly between shooting or passing a ball back to the player who passed it to him.

Variation—The same drill, only a defender is added to the drill. A moves about and can call for a ball from any of the outside players, that is, B, C, D, E, and F. If A cannot get a clear shot on the goal, he passes back to the player who passed to him.

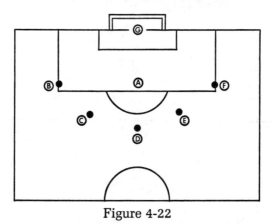

Figure 4-22

Drill 4-23 Rebound Soccer

No. of players—Five on five, or six on six

Equipment—Two rebound surfaces at each end of one-half of a soccer field, i.e. picnic tables, benches, etc.

Explanation—A regular game of soccer is played only the play is continuous on one half of a soccer field. When a goal is scored players can score again at the same goal. The only time play is stopped is when the ball goes out of bounds. It is brought back into play by the conventional throw in.

Purpose—Players practice following up their shots on the goal.

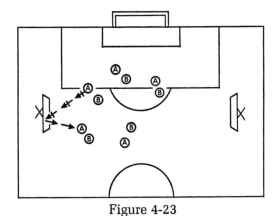

Figure 4-23

Drill 4-24 Win It Back and Shoot

No. of players—Ten per drill group

Explanation—The six A players are passers and the four B players try to intercept the ball and quickly shoot at the goal. A players try to pass the ball inside the eighteen-yard area and the Bs try to

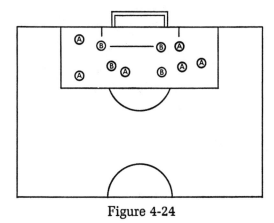

Figure 4-24

intercept a pass and get a quick shot off. As can only pass, they
cannot shoot. When a ball goes in the goal or out of play, a new
ball is thrown in.

Purpose—As simulate a defending team that has just won a ball
back in their own penalty area. The B players are forwards, practicing an immediate chase to win the ball back after it is lost. In
match play, many goals are scored from winning the ball back near
the goal.

Drill 4-25 Five-on-Four in the Penalty Area (No Diagram)

No. of players—Nine per drill group

Equipment—A supply of soccer balls.

Explanation—The defending team includes three field players and
one goalkeeper. The attacking team includes five attacking players.
The five attackers attempt to score on the four defenders. All play
is inside the penalty area. If a ball is kicked out of the penalty area,
another ball is immediately thrown to one of the five attacking
players.

Purpose—Attacking players practice quick shooting while coping
with the pressure of the defenders. This is a drill used to promote
frequent and quick shooting opportunities.

Drill 4-26 Same Side "1-touch" Shooting

No. of players—Four per drill group

Distance—A to B—20 to 25 yards, C to D—20 to 25 yards.

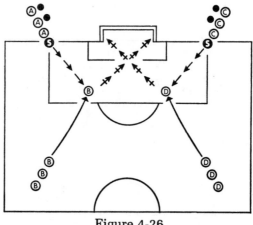

Figure 4-26

Explanation—On a signal, A and C each pass a ball across the corner of the outer goal area line as seen in the diagram. B and D run to their respective balls and "1-touch" shoot at the goal. A gets in the back of B's line and B gets in the back of A's line. C gets in the back of D's line and D gets in back of C's line.

Purpose—Players B and D practice "1-touch" shooting.

Drill 4-27 Cross Over "1-touch" Shooting

No. of players—Four per drill group

Distance—A to B—20 to 25 yards, C to D—20 to 25 yards

Explanation—On a signal, A and C pass their balls across the goal area, as seen in the diagram. B and D run to their respective balls and "1-touch" shoot at the goal.

Rotation order—A gets in the back of B's line and B gets in back of A's line. C gets in D's line and D gets in back of C's line.

Purpose—Players B and D practice "1-touch" shooting.

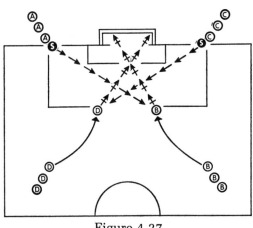

Figure 4-27

Drill 4-28 Wall and Shoot

No. of players—Four per drill group

Distance—A to B—20 to 25 yards, C to D—20 to 25 yards.

Explanation—A passes to B. B dribbles diagonally forward and passes back to A. A then wall passes back to B and B shoots at the goal. C and D repeat the same procedure.

Rotation order—A gets in the back of B's line and B gets in back of A's line. C gets in back of D's line and D gets in the back of C's line.

Purpose—Players practice wall passing and shooting.

Variation—A passes to D. D passes back to A. A wall passes to D and D "1-touch" shoots at the goal. C and D perform the same procedure.

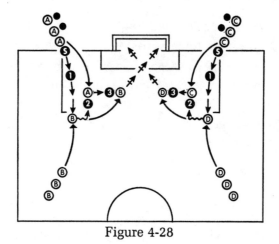

Figure 4-28

Drill 4-29 Exchange and Shoot

No. of players—Four per drill group

Distance—A to B—20 to 25 yards, C to D—20 to 25 yards

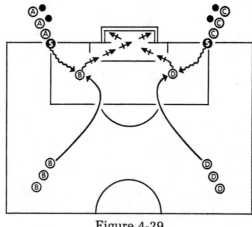

Figure 4-29

Explanation—A dribbles straight ahead a few times and then dribbles toward the center of the field. A leaves the ball for B. B makes a loop run, collects the ball, and dribbles behind A. B shoots at the goal. C and D repeat the same procedure.

Purpose—A and B practice a maneuver used to get player B free for a shot at the goal.

Drill 4–30 Give and Go

No. of players—Four per drill group

Distance—A to B—20 to 25 yards, C to D—20 to 25 yards

Explanation—B passes to A and A comes forward to meet the ball. A "1-touches" it back to B and, immediately after passing to B, breaks toward the goal. B passes to A and A shoots at the goal. C and D then repeats the same procedure.

Purpose—Players practice a give and go maneuver used to get free for a shot at the goal.

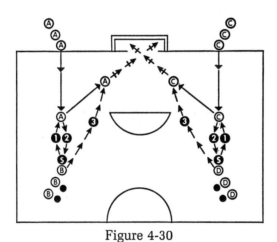

Figure 4-30

Drill 4-31 Loop Run

No. of players—Four per drill group

Distance—A to B—20 to 25 yards, C to D—20 to 25 yards.

Explanation—A runs toward B and quickly changes direction toward the goal. B passes to A and A shoots at the goal. C and D perform the same procedure.

Purpose—Players practice a loop run maneuver used by player A to get himself free to receive a pass and a shot at the goal.

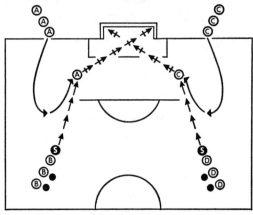

Figure 4-31

Drill 4-32 Back, Cross, Shoot

No. of players—Four per drill group

Distance—A to B—20 to 25 yards, C to D—20 to 25 yards

Explanation—A passes back to B. B crosses the ball directly in front of D and D shoots at the goal.

    After D shoots at the goal, a second ball is started from position C. C passes to D, D crosses, and B shoots at the goal.

Purpose—Players practice a back pass and crossing a ball for a shot at the goal.

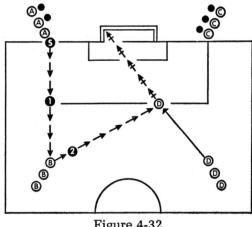

Figure 4-32

Drill 4–33 Back, Cross, and Wall

No. of players—Four per drill group

Distance—A to B—20 to 25 yards, C to D—20 to 25 yards.

Explanation—C crosses back to B. B passes straight forward to A and A sends a wall pass for D to shoot at the goal.

After D shoots at the goal, a second ball is put into play by player A. A passes to D and D passes forward to C. C wall passes and B comes forward to take a shot at the goal.

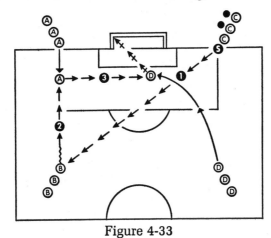

Figure 4-33

Drill 4-34 Back Pass, Exchange, and Shoot

No. of players—Four per drill group

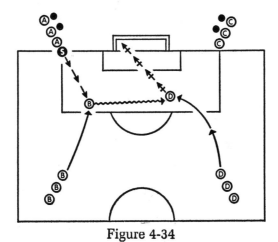

Figure 4-34

Distance—A to B—20 to 25 yards, C to D—20 to 25 yards

Explanation—A passes to B. B dribbles straight across the field. D makes a loop run, turns toward B, collects the ball B left for him and shoots at the goal.

After D shoots at the goal, another ball is started from position C. C passes to D. D leaves the ball off for player B and B shoots at the goal.

Purpose—Players practice an exchange maneuver used to free a player for a shot at the goal.

Drill 4-35 Back Pass, Dribble, Overlap, Shoot

No. of players—Four per drill group

Distance—A to B—20 to 25 yards, C to D—20 to 25 yards

Explanation—A passes diagonally back to D. D collects the ball and dribbles across the field. B overlaps D. D passes to B, who shoots at the goal.

After B shoots at the goal, C starts a second ball. C passes to B. B dribbles diagonally across. D overlaps B. B passes to D and D shoots at the goal.

Purpose—This is a three-man maneuver used to free a player for a shot at the goal.

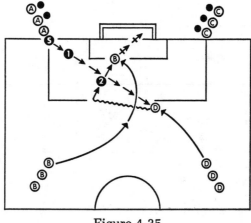

Figure 4-35

5

Defense and Tackling

When a player has time to control a ball, he has open space. In other words, when a player receives a ball, no opponent is in his immediate vicinity. Attackers are seeking open space while defenders try to deny open space. The more proficient a player is at controlling a ball, the more time he has to use the space available to him. In today's game, tight marking limits the time available for a player to control the ball and this also limits the time he has to make his next move.

In lieu of this, "1-touch" play, the ability to think ahead and quick counterattacking should be incorporated into the training program to prepare defending players. Defenders need a predetermined plan of action so that they can move the ball forward quickly once it is repossessed. A variety of clearing drills are included in this chapter for this reason. In some of these drills, a target area can be set up on the field. Once a defender repossesses a ball, he should quickly get the ball to the target area for quick counterattack possibilities.

Today, defenders are sometimes called on to attack and likewise strikers are called on to defend. Goals are frequently scored because a forward makes a tackle and quickly counterattacks. For this reason, it is important that forwards should participate in drills that involve the skills of tackling and defensive tactics. By the same token, defenders should participate in so-called attack drills. Today many coaches are encouraging their defenders to overlap and come forward for a shot on the goal when an opportunity develops.

Immediate pursuit from an attacker who lost possession of a ball should be drilled until it is an automatic reaction. A player who has lost a ball should immediately think about moving back and positioning himself in front of the player who previously won the ball. At this point he should restrict possible passing angles and wait for his chance to make a tackle. Further, he jockeys the player in possession of the ball hoping that his opponents will make a square pass that may be picked off by one of his teammates. This points out a strong need for all players to participate in defensive exercises. All players need the skills necessary to tackle and the skills needed to repossess balls.

When basic techniques of tackling have been learned, drills with match-like action should be introduced. One on one, two on one, and three on two in a restricted lane. This is an effective setting for polishing defensive techniques and skills. One on one can be played in a grid ten yards by twenty yards, two on one in a grid fifteen by thirty yards and a three on two in a grid forty by twenty yards.

The reader should refer to the first six drills in this chapter for further information about grid drills including 2, 3, 4, and 5 players.

A coach can increase or decrease the pressure in a grid by increasing or decreasing the width of the grid. To increase pressure on defenders make the grid wider, add pressure on the attackers, shorten the width of the grid.

In this chapter, you will find a variety of tackling and defensive drills that are selected to help improve a player's defensive tactical abilities.

The following is a list to be used as a basis for developing defensive and tackling drills:

1. technique or skill drills involving tackling
2. drills involving jockeying
3. drills involving sweeping
4. drills involving preparation against quick switching of the ball.

5. drills involving funnelling and falling back

6. drills involving establishing balance, depth, and width to a defense

7. drills involving limiting passing opportunities

8. drills involving communications among players

9. drills involving delaying an attack

10. drills involving defense and quick counterattacking

These are just some of the basic concepts used in developing defensive technique and defensive tactical drills.

Drill 5-1 Alley Grid Drill

No. of players—Two per drill group

Distance—Cones or flags form a ten-yard by twenty-yard alley.

Explanation—The defender kicks the ball to A. A tries to beat the defender by dribbling over the opposite endline while at the same time the defender tries to contain A and force him to the sideline and make the tackle.

Purpose—Defensive players practice containing and tackling in a limited area.

Variation—The same drill only the defender is restricted to making his tackle with his weak foot.

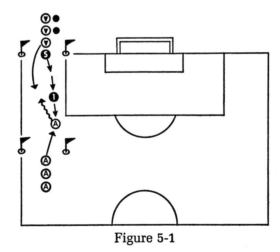

Figure 5-1

Drill 5-2 Two-on-one Alley Grid Drill

No. of players—Three per drill group

Distance—Cones form a fifteen- by thirty-yard alley grid.

Explanation—The defender passes to either A or B. The objective of A and B is to beat the defender and to cross over the opposite endline. The defender should position himself close to the player with the ball and at the same time be in a position where he can cut off any pass.

Purpose—Defensive player practices positioning himself to best handle a two against one situation in a limited area.

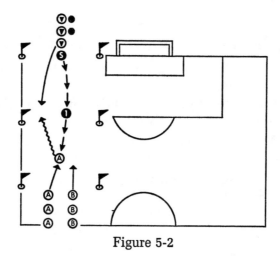

Figure 5-2

Drill 5-3 Two-on-one Catch Up

No. of players—Three per drill group

Distance—Cones form a twenty-yard by forty-yard rectangle.

Explanation—The defender at the far end of the grid kicks the ball to player A. This defender then runs and tries to prevent A from dribbling to the far end of the grid. To add pressure on A and to make A move quickly toward the far end of the grid, have another defender pursue A from behind. This extra defender must remain between the cones until the ball is first touched by player A.

Purpose—Defenders practice containing and tackling and attackers practice moving the ball quickly up the field.

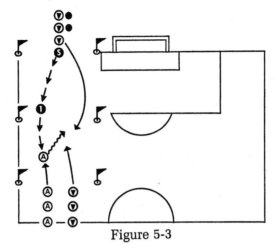

Figure 5-3

Drill 5-4 Forcing a Two-on-one

No. of players—Three per drill group

Equipment—Six cones or flags

Distance—The six cones form a twenty-yard by forty-yard grid.

Explanation—One defender stands with his hand on one of the middle cones. Play starts on a signal (whistle). On the signal, A tries to dribble to the opposite end of the grid. The whistle is also a signal for the defender at the far end of the grid to run and attempt to force player A close to the defender with his hand on the cone. The defender touching the cone cannot leave the cone until he is

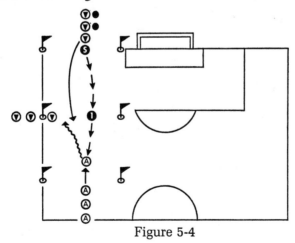

Figure 5-4

touched by the other defender. When he is tagged he can leave the cone and team up to help the other defender make the tackle.

Purpose—Defensive players practice forcing a two-on-one situation in their favor.

Drill 5-5 Two-on-one Delayed Pressure

No. of players—Four per drill group

Distance—Six cones form a twenty-yard by forty-yard rectangle, as seen in the diagram.

Explanation—The defender at the far end of the grid kicks the ball to player A. After kicking the ball, this defender immediately runs and tries to prevent A from getting to the far end of the grid. The defender and player B in the middle of the grid are not allowed to move until A first touches the ball. B tries to get into position for a pass from A or he tries to move to a position that will help A move the ball forward.

Purpose—Defending players practice tackling and containing skills in a two-on-two situation.

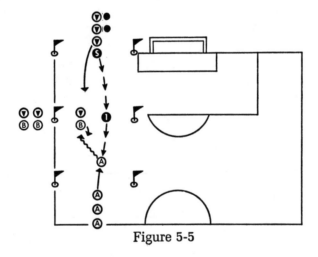

Figure 5-5

Drill 5-6 Three-on-two Alley Grid Drill

No. of players—Five per drill group

Distance—Cones form a twenty- by forty-alley grid.

Explanation—Play starts when one of the defenders kicks the ball to the A players. One of the three A players gathers the ball and starts to move toward the goal. The objective for the three A players is to beat the two defenders and to dribble the ball over the end-line. The closest defender to the ball marks player A with the ball. The other defenders trail and try to intercept passes and to prevent a breakthrough. When a breakthrough occurs, defenders reverse their roles. The front defender moves back and supports while the other defender marks the player with the ball.

Purpose—The defenders practice marking and sweeping for each other. Defensive players practice running goal side when they are beaten.

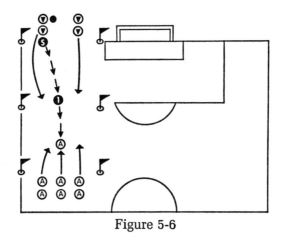

Figure 5-6

Drill 5-7 Contain and Tackle (No Diagram)

No. of players—Two per drill group

Explanation—Defenders line up in a single file beside the goal post. Attackers line up in a single file behind the center circle. The first person in each of the two lines play one-on-one. The defender contains and slows down the attacker until the defender backs up to the penalty area front line. When he crosses this line, the defender must make his tackle.

Up until the time the attacker crosses the eighteen-yard line, the defender backs up. The only time the defender can attempt to tackle is when the attacker makes a serious mistake, such as pushing the ball too far in front.

Purpose—Defenders practice patience and containing an attacker until he makes a mistake. Further, the defenders practices tackling when it is vital to do so.

Drill 5-8 Keep from Turning

No. of players—Two per drill group

Explanation—The defender stands two feet away from A's back, facing A's back. A is facing away from the goal. On a whistle, A players try to turn the ball and get a shot at the goal. The defensive players try to prevent A from turning the ball and getting a shot at the goal.

Purpose—Defensive players practice keeping an attacker from turning and facing the goal.

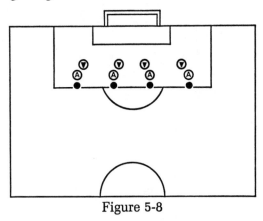

Figure 5-8

Drill 5-9 Volley Clearing (No Diagram)

No. of players—Two per drill group

Equipment—A supply of soccer balls

Explanation—Defenders practice volley kicking balls that are served from many different angles:

1. from over the head
2. from straight on
3. from right and from the left

Clearing is made with the knee up and the foot down to avoid being called for dangerous play.

Purpose—Defenders practice a clearing skill while avoiding dangerous play calls.

Drill 5-10 One-on-one Jockey

No. of players—Two per drill group

Explanation—A tries to dribble the ball down the middle of the field and get a shot on goal. The defensive player is given instructions as to which direction he is to force player A to go. For example, the coach secretly tells the first defender "right." Play begins on the whistle. The defensive player sprints up the field and attempts to force A to his right. The second group begins before the first group has finished playing.

Purpose—Players practice one-on-one attacking techniques.

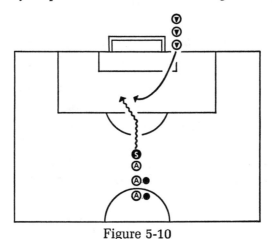

Figure 5-10

Drill 5-11 One-on-one Around the Goal

No. of players—Three per drill group

Explanation—On a signal (whistle), A tries to dribble in for a shot at the goal. On the same signal, the defender runs around the goal and back toward A to prevent A from shooting.

Purpose—Defenders practice tackling and protecting the baseline.

Variation—Use the same drill, only place another attacking player on the far outer corner of the penalty area line to receive a possible pass from A if the situation warrants such a pass.

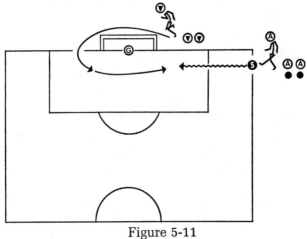

Figure 5-11

Drill 5-12 One-on-one Daylight

No. of players—Three per drill group

Explanation—A starts dribbling parallel to the goal line along the penalty area line. A uses feints and change-of-pace runs to get clear for a shot. Defenders attempt to stay between the ball and the goal to prevent a shot.

Purpose—Defensive players practice tackling and defensive skills. Attackers practice feints and change-of-pace runs to get free for a shot at the goal.

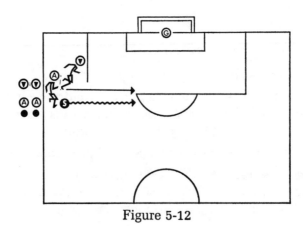

Figure 5-12

Drill 5-13 Close in Clearing

No. of players—Three per drill group

Distances—B to the defender—three yards

Explanation—A kicks the ball on the ground or in the air to B. B "1-touches" the ball toward the goal. The defender's job is to clear the ball.

B should be instructed to kick the ball hard, but not to blast it at the defender. B should be realistic. B can increase how hard he hits the ball as the defender improves his ability to handle the kicks.

Purpose—Defenders practice clearing balls in a tight, close situation.

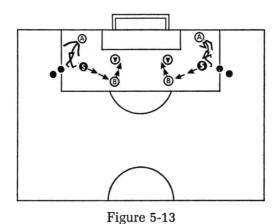

Figure 5-13

Drill 5-14 Get in Front

No. of players—Nine per drill group

Explanation—A faces the goal and the defender faces away from the goal. Balls are placed five yards in front of player A. On a signal (whistle), players try to get control of the ball. The defender should get goal side and face the attacking player.

Purpose—Players improve their physical fitness and defensive skills. A players practice their attacking skills.

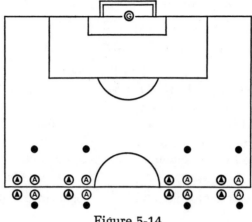

Figure 5-14

Drill 5-15 One-on-one Pressure Tackling

No. of players—Three per drill group

Explanation—A attacks the defender by dribbling directly at him. Immediately after the defender wins the ball or is beaten another attacker attacks the same defender. After a defender faces four or more attackers in a row, a new defender takes his place.

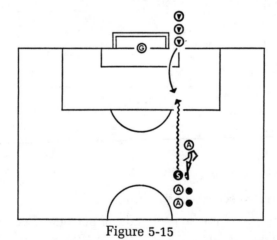

Figure 5-15

Drill 5-16 Get Up and Go

No. of players—Four per drill group

Distance—B and the defender—fifteen yards apart

Explanation—B and the defender are in a sitting position facing away from the center of the field. A kicks the ball between the defender and player B. Then, on a signal, B and the defender try to get control of the ball. B tries to get a shot at the goal and the defender tries to turn the ball back and take it over the half-field line.

Purpose—Players practice attack and defending skills in a one-on-one situation.

Variation—When a defender or the goalkeeper gets control of the ball, he quickly moves out and starts a quick counterattack. Defenders can be timed to see how long it takes them to get the ball over the opponent's goal line. When, and if, A players lose the ball to the defenders, they should immediately try to prevent the counterattack.

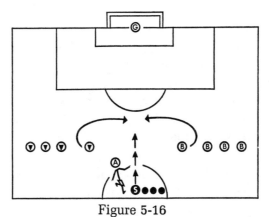

Figure 5-16

Drill 5-17 Goal Area Clearing

No. of players—Four defenders and an unlimited number of A players

Explanation—A players try to chip balls into the goal from outside the eighteen-yard line. The four defenders try to clear the balls. Defenders are instructed not to let the balls touch on the ground inside the goal area.

Purpose—Defenders practice clearing chipped balls.

Variation—A players kick ground balls at the goal and the defenders clear these balls.

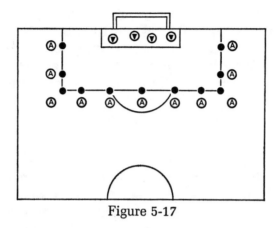

Figure 5-17

Drill 5-18 One-on-one Goalside and Quick Counterattack

No. of players—Three per drill group

Explanation—On a signal, A dribbles toward the goal for a shot. The defensive player attempts to get goal side of A and stop him. If the defender gains control of the ball, he immediately kicks it into the center circle. If A succeeds in getting a shot on goal and the goalkeeper saves the ball, the goalkeeper throws the ball to the defender. The defender quickly trys to kick the ball into the center circle.

Purpose—Defensive players practice defensive skills and clearing the ball to a designated area. The goalkeeper and the defender practice a quick counterattack combination.

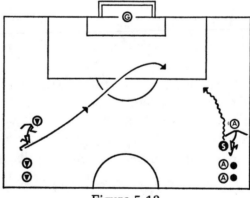

Figure 5-18

Drill 5-19 Delay and Prevent

No. of players—Four per drill group

Explanation—The defensive player kicks the ball to player A. As soon as the ball is kicked, the defender runs around the goal, back onto the field and attempts to delay and prevent A from getting off a shot at the goal. A has the option to pass off to B or to keep the ball and dribble on. If A passes to B, the goalkeeper comes out and tries to cut off the pass or to take on player B.

Purpose—Defensive players practice delaying tactics. The goalkeeper practices working together with a defender.

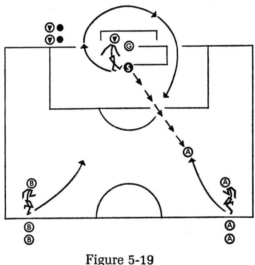

Figure 5-19

Drill 5-20 Quick Clear and Counterattack

No. of players—Four per drill group

Distance—A to B—10 yards, B to C—10 to 15 yards.

Explanation—Player A throws a ball to player B. A throws the ball toward and to the side of player B so that the position of the ball is two feet off the ground when it reaches B. Balls are thrown hard so that player B cannot take a step to get in front of the ball. B must clear the ball on a "1-touch" basis to player C. B should clear the ball with the inside of the foot. C collects each ball and quickly sends it to D for a quick counterattack.

Purpose—Defensive players practice clearing balls with the inside of the foot to a target.

Variation—A throws ten balls in rapid succession for B to clear. Vary which side the balls are thrown to keep B guessing.

Variation—The same drill only the balls are thrown at B's head.

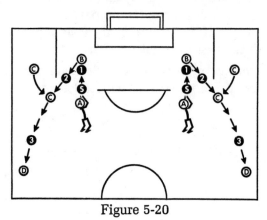

Figure 5-20

Drill 5-21 Hot Seat

No. of players—Seven per drill group

Explanation—A, B, and C in turn shoot a ball at the goal. Each defender stays on the hot seat until nine balls are shot at the goal. Each time the defender or the goalkeeper gets possession of the ball, he starts a quick counterattack. The ball is passed to the defender outside the eighteen-yard line.

Figure 5-21

Purpose—Defenders and the goalkeeper work together to keep balls out of the goal. Defenders practice a quick counterattack combination.

Drill 5-22 Scramble

No. of players—Eight per drill group

Explanation—Each defender is instructed to cover a specific attacker. A, B, C, and D start dribbling when the whistle blows. A, B, C, and D should mingle and criss-cross with their balls, trying to confuse their respective defenders. When they reach the vicinity of the defenders, they should sprint off for a shot at the goal.

Purpose—Defenders practice tackling skills in a crowded area.

Variation—The same drill, only set up target areas for defenders. Once they get control of the balls, they send them to the target area.

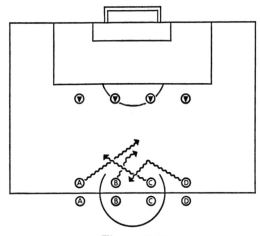

Figure 5-22

6

Goalkeeping

The goalkeeper has a dual role. On the one hand he is the commanding general of the defense, on the other he is the initiator of the attack.

A goalkeeper sometimes must depend on his instincts to direct him. When his instincts are wrong he may look foolish, but more times he is right and he will look like a hero.

No matter how a ball is caught, a goalkeeper must make every effort to get his body behind the ball in case it goes through his hands. In this way it will hit his body and he will get a second chance to gain possession of it.

As the ball is approaching the goalkeeper, he must keep his eyes on the ball. When it makes impact with his hands, he absorbs the force by relaxing his arms and bringing the ball to his body. He should treat a caught ball like he would handle a baby in an unruly crowd.

Quickness of movement can help a goalkeeper to get his body behind the approaching ball. It's easiest for a goalkeeper to catch a ball that is approaching chest high, especially if he gets into position with his body behind the ball. Sometimes a goalkeeper cannot get his body behind the ball and must rely on his emergency skills such as diving, punching, and deflecting. A goalkeeper who can quickly move into position will not need to use these emergency skills as frequently as will a slower-moving goalkeeper. Spectators usually judge a goalkeeper's ability by the number of spectacular flying dives he makes, but this is an indication of poor technique. It should be noted that a goalkeeper who must dive frequently to catch balls is one who is out of position. Good goalkeepers make their jobs look easy and not spectacular.

A goalkeeper can leave the goal to gather a ball that he thinks he has a good chance of getting. At other times, he can come out of the goal to narrow the angle of an attacker who has slipped through the last defender. In both instances, the goalkeeper must be decisive.

The goalkeeper should follow the ball from the kicker's foot to the goalkeeper's hands. Many players have the ability to kick the ball so it will drop, swerve, or rise, therefore, if the goalkeeper takes his eyes off the ball, he may find that is not in the position he had anticipated.

The goalkeeper should assess each ball kicked to him with the following questions in mind:

1. What is the goalkeeper's position on the field?
2. What is the relative position of his teammates?
3. Where is the ball coming from?
4. How high is the ball?
5. How fast is it coming?
6. How far out from the goal is the ball being kicked from?
7. How much spin is on the ball?
8. Is the ball curving, dipping, or hooking?
9. How should he handle the ball when it arrives—catch it, dive and catch it, punch it, deflect it, etc.

Each of the above questions must be answered in a flash. The goalkeeper does not have time to hesitate. Through a variety of drills and playing experiences, a player learns to react instinctively to the situation.

NARROWING THE ANGLE

A goalkeeper, by moving several yards off the goal line to meet an oncoming player, improves his chances of getting control of the ball. By advancing toward the oncoming player, a goalkeeper lessens the chance that he will need to resort to emergency skills such as diving, punching, or tipping.

How far a goalkeeper advances is determined by calculating the anticipated distance you expect the forward will shoot. At thirty yards out, a goalkeeper need only to advance a few yards. But, for a shot from near the eighteen-yard line, the goalkeeper needs to advance further because of the time factor necessary to save a ball closer to the goal. This does not mean that a goalkeeper rushes out recklessly every time. He moves forward quickly in control. He is constantly reminding himself to get ready to retreat in case the ball is chipped.

While advancing, he should be prepared for a low shot at the goal. To accommodate a low shot, he should advance or retreat, depending on the situation, keeping his body in a low position.

It is very simple to set up drills to learn how to narrow the angle. Seven or more players are placed in different positions in an arch around the penalty area. Players are instructed to shoot hard at the goal. Occasionally, a ball should be chipped to keep the goalkeeper honest. After each shot the goalkeeper and the coach analyze whether or not his position was correct on the previous shot. Soon the goalkeeper will get a feel for assuming the correct position, or how far he needs to advance for shots taken at different distances and angles.

Next, move the shooters closer to the goal. In this manner, the goalkeeper can get experience at advancing and narrowing the angle of a ball being shot at a closer distance. The idea is to change the distance of the shot so that the goalkeeper can develop a personal feel for the distance he should advance toward the shooter. How far a goalkeeper should advance differs from one goalkeeper to another. This is because of the physical differences and the different styles of goalkeepers. Each goalkeeper should be aware of his individual ability in handling balls from various distances and heights.

A short goalkeeper may be required to come out farther, but a tall goalkeeper would not have to advance as far.

Finally, a coach can vary the distance of the shooters, as seen in the diagram, so that the goalkeeper must change his position each time to accommodate and react to various distances. Before long these drills will help a goalkeeper to get a feel for narrowing the angle for shots coming from various distances.

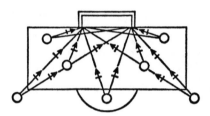

The preceding paragraphs suggest the general responsibility of a goalkeeper in match play. Each of these responsibilities is the basis for developing drills to reinforce an aspect of goalkeeper's effectiveness. The following is a list of specific technical responsibilities you can use to develop a drill program for your goalkeeper.

The first step is to teach the skill. Next incorporate the skill in a pressure drill and finally use the skill on a functional drill. In this way the technique or skill will be meaningfully reinforced and relate to what happens in match play.

In pressure training balls should be served at a rapid rate so players learn to perform in an automatic fashion. Functional training centers around the position the player is assigned. Example: One goalkeeper and one defender against one attacker.

In practicing special situations, start by staging or setting up a special situation. Next, designate the location of the starting position of the goalkeeper. Also suggest what his first action should entail. The special situation is then executed and when it succeeds or fails, repeat it for reinforcement or for correction.

The following are special situations a coach can stage in a practice session:

1. corner kicks
2. penalty kicks—direct and indirect

3. goal kicks
4. handling throw-ins close to the goal
5. distributing the ball

What qualities does a coach look for in selecting a player to play in the goal? Some of these qualities are inherited while others can be improved by hard work and playing experience. To name a few:

reaction time

agility

anticipation

courage

recovery speed

speed of movement

Individuals are born with a capacity for each of these qualities. Potential parameters for improvement in these qualities differ for each individual. Experts tell us that of all these personal qualities, speed of movement can be improved to the greatest extent. Thus, more time should be spent in improving this quality. The other personal qualities are usually developed through game experience and concomitantly improved through the overall training process.

For the sake of clarity and simplicity, the goalkeeper drills in this book are arranged under the following headings:

Drills for individual goalkeepers

Drills for two goalkeepers

Drills for three goalkeepers

Pressure training drills

Functional training drills

Special situation drills.

DRILLS FOR INDIVIDUAL GOALKEEPERS

Drill 6-2 Drills for Individual Goalkeepers (No Diagram)

- Bend at the waist, pass a ball between the legs in a figure eight, then circle the ball around both legs.

- Grasp a ball between the legs, with one hand behind the ball and the other in front of the ball. Quickly change hands and repeat the same procedure.

- In a prone position, with the arms extended in front, tap or hand dribble a ball with both hands.

- In a supine position, chest pass the ball high, roll 360 degrees, and catch the ball before it hits the ground.

- Close your eyes and throw a ball up and catch it. As you improve, increase the height it is thrown.

- While standing, throw a ball in the air, turn 360 degrees, and catch the ball. Repeat, only this time turn two times before you catch the ball.

- Bounce the ball off your toes and try to catch it before it hits the ground.

- Hand juggle two balls.

- Hand juggle three balls.

- Bounce a ball between the legs, turn, and try to catch it before it hits the ground.

- Stand behind the goal, throw the ball over the goal, and try to catch it after one bounce. Run around the outside of the goalpost.

- Repeat the preceding drill, only try to catch the ball before it hits the ground.

- Practice falling and diving from a sitting, kneeling, or standing position with a ball in your hands.

- In a standing position roll a ball back between your legs, turn, and dive on it.

- In a standing position, throw a ball in the air, performing a forward roll, and catch the ball before it hits the ground.

- Repeat the preceding drill only perform a back roll and catch a ball before it hits the ground.

- Punt and drop kick a ball into the net.

- Throw a ball high in the air, catch it, and quickly punt it. This is good practice for quick counterattacking.

- Throw balls near the goal line attempting to knock cones down that are set up in the center circle.

- Place five balls ten feet apart and in a line. Try to dive and gather the balls with the least number of steps. Move the balls further apart and repeat the same procedure.

- Place five balls on the goal line inside the goalpost. Pick the first ball up and tap it on the crossbar three times. On the fourth time, jump and dunk it over the crossbar basketball style with both hands. Add more balls to this drill when the goalkeeper's physical condition improves.

- Make a ten-foot square with four balls, one ball at each corner of the square. Dive for a ball, sprint, and place it the center of the square. Then repeat the same for the other three balls. Make the square larger as the goalkeeper improves.

- From inside the goal, throw a ball in the air and punch it up and out for distance.

DRILLS FOR TWO GOALKEEPERS

Drill 6-3 Drills for Two Goalkeepers (No Diagrams)

- Two goalkeepers are situated ten yards apart. They drop kick a ball back and forth. They start drop kicking it easy and later kick it harder.

- The same as the preceding drill only the goalkeepers try to catch the ball without making a noise when it hits their hands.

- Two goalkeepers stand face to face, approximately two feet apart. These goalkeepers throw a ball back and forth. The ball is thrown chest high and easy. When the ball hits the chest the receiver curls his arms and pulls the ball to the chest.

- Repeat the preceding drill only the eyes of the receiving goalkeeper are closed. When the goalkeeper feels the ball hit his chest, he curls his arms and pulls the ball into his chest.

- Two goalkeepers stand five yards apart. They throw a ball back and forth. All throwing and catching is done with one hand. When the players become proficient, increase the speed of the throws.

- Two goalkeepers stand five yards apart with their hands over their heads. With both hands, they throw a ball back and forth. When throwing, they aim at the other player's hands.

- Two goalkeepers practice diving and falling. One goalkeeper throws and the other dives. Balls are thrown within reach, and off to one side, of the other goalkeeper:

First—from a sitting position

Second—from a kneeling position

Third—from a squatting position

Fourth—from a standing position

These drills should be closely supervised by the coach, especially in the early stage of training. Correct technique and safety should be stressed.

- One goalkeeper throws to another goalkeeper. Balls are thrown so that the receiving goalkeeper must dive over an obstacle, such as a cone, to catch a ball. Start with one cone and add another cone when improvement is indicated. Use mats or a saw-dust pit to cushion the fall of the goalkeeper.
- Two goalkeepers practice tipping high outside balls. The server throws balls high and outside to the other goalkeeper. For balls going to the right side, the goalkeeper should tip them with the left hand. Balls on the left outside side should be tipped with the right hand. However, in tipping low balls, use the hand that the ball is approaching. For example, if the ball is approaching from the right side, use the right hand.
- Log roll and dive—One goalkeeper performs a log roll, gets back to his feet, and dives to catch a ball thrown by the other goalkeeper.
- Two goalkeepers are two feet apart. One of these goalkeepers is facing the other goalkeeper's back. The goalkeeper facing the other goalkeeper's back rolls a ball between the other goalkeeper's legs. As soon as the front goalkeeper sees the ball coming through his legs, he leaps and gathers it.
- Reaction drill—Two goalkeepers face each other about five yards apart. One of the goalkeepers drop kicks the ball to the other goalkeeper. Immediately after he kicks it, he turns 360 degrees and gets ready to receive the ball coming back from the other goalkeeper. Each goalkeeper turns 360 degrees after he kicks the ball.

DRILLS FOR THREE AND FOUR GOALKEEPERS

Drill 6-4 Forward Roll and Look (No Diagram)

No. of players—Three per drill

Explanation—One of the three goalkeepers is the server. One of the two other goalkeepers performs a forward roll and comes up to his feet looking for the ball. The ball is dropped or thrown by the server. The performing goalkeeper gathers the ball, throws it back to the server and gets behind the other goalkeeper. The next goalkeeper in line repeats the same procedure and play continues.

Drill 6-5 Goalkeeper Keep Away (No Diagram)

No. of players—Three or four goalkeepers

Explanation—Inside the penalty area, three or four goalkeepers play a game of keep away. Two against one or two against two. The goalkeeper in possession of the ball is restricted to three steps and then he must throw the ball. If the ball hits the ground it is given to the other team. Balls can be wrestled away from an opponent if he holds it, but when the game gets bogged down, it is stopped and restarted.

Drill 6-6 Musical Balls (No Diagram)

No. of players—Three per drill group

Explanation—Two balls are placed inside the center circle. Three goalkeepers shuffle or side step around the perimeter of the circle. On a signal (whistle), each goalkeeper sprints to get control of the ball. Play continues until the two balls are in the possession of two of the three players.

- A drill for practicing breakaway situations, that is, when an attacker beats the last defender and is facing the goalkeeper in a one-on-one situation—The goalkeeper is on his knees and the server is four or five feet away. Balls are kicked with the side of the foot. Balls are kicked so that the goalkeeper has a chance of catching them.
- Two goalkeepers stand two or three feet from each other. One goalkeeper throws a ball to the other goalkeeper and as

soon as it touches the receiver's hands the thrower attempts to bat the ball away. The receiving goalkeeper should immediately cuddle the ball and protect it. Players take turns receiving a ball. This is a good drill to make goalkeepers cover a ball up immediately after receiving it.

• The goalkeeper is lying on his side facing the server. The server is ten feet away. Balls are rolled to the goalkeepers feet. The goalkeeper turns his body without getting up and catches the ball.

• Two goalkeepers sit facing each other. Their legs are straight and the soles of their feet are touching each other. On a signal each bounces his ball along side of the other goalkeeper. Each goalkeeper bounces his ball on his right side. Each then tries to recover his partner's ball before it hits the ground a second time.

• From behind the goal a server throws balls over the goal toward the goalkeeper. The goalkeeper jumps high and punches the balls back over the goal with two fists.

• From the baseline, two goalkeepers compete to see who can punt the longest ball.

Drill 6-7 Tap and Dunk Contest

No. of players—Three per drill group

Explanation—Three goalkeepers compete in the following exercise. Three balls are placed on the eighteen-yard line for each of the three goalkeepers. The three goalkeepers line up on the six-yard

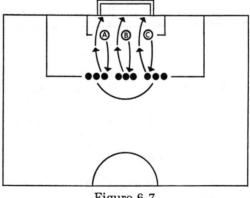

Figure 6-7

line as seen in the diagram. On a whistle, each player sprints to the penalty area line, picks up a ball, and races to the goal post. He then jumps three times touching his ball each time he jumps on the goalpost or crossbar. On the fourth jump he dunks the ball over the crossbar. He repeats the same procedure with the second and third balls. The six-yard line is the finish line.

This is a good fitness activity and is used to improve the quickness of the goalkeeper.

PRESSURE DRILLS

Drill 6-8 Right and Left Diving (No Diagram)

No. of players—Two per drill group

Explanation—Two goalkeepers face each other with a distance of five yards between them. One goalkeeper serves balls on the ground to the other goalkeeper with his feet. The receiving goalkeeper immediately catches and then rolls each ball back to the server's feet. Play is rapid. The balls are kicked in a "1-touch" fashion. Each ball is kicked so that the receiving goalkeeper catches and falls or dives for each ball.

The receiving goalkeeper can start this drill on his knees and, after catching a series of balls, he can move to his feet.

Drill 6-9 Hop Over and Dive (No Diagram)

No. of players—Two per drill group

Explanation—Two goalkeepers face each other with a distance of four yards between them. A ball is placed alongside one of the goalkeepers. He hops over the ball three times with his feet together. After the third hop, the server throws a ball toward the side where the goalkeeper started the drill. The ball should be thrown in a manner that will make the goalkeeper dive to get possession of the ball.

Drill 6-10 Tag and Dive (No Diagram)

No. of players—Two per drill group

Explanation—Two cones are placed four yards apart. The goalkeeper starts the drill with one hand touching one of the cones.

The server throws a ball in the direction of the other cone with his hands. The goalkeeper dives, gathers the ball, and throws it back to the receiver. He immediately runs back to touch the cone at the starting position. Repeat the same procedure.

Drill 6-11 Tipping and Punching (No Diagram)

No. of players—Two per drill group

Explanation—Punching—From a kneeling position a goalkeeper punches balls with both fist. Balls are fed to him in rapid succession. The balls are punched in the same direction from which they came. Repeat the same drill standing.

Tipping—Repeat the same procedure, only balls should be served to the side of the goalkeeper. Balls coming from the left should be tipped to the right. Balls coming from the right should be tipped to the left.

This drill can be performed in a sitting, kneeling, and standing position.

Drill 6-12 Follow the Server (No Diagram)

No. of players—Two per drill group

Explanation—A goalkeeper performs a forward roll in the direction of the server. As he comes out of his forward roll, the server throws the ball to him. He throws the ball back to the server, immediately performs a forward roll, and repeats the same procedure.

Drill 6-13 Quick Tip (No Diagram)

Explanation—Balls are thrown at a goalkeeper from a distance of ten feet while the goalkeeper is in the goal. The balls are thrown just above the goalkeepers head in a two-hand chest pass fashion. The balls should be thrown in rapid succession with speed so that the goalkeeper only has enough time to tip the ball over the crossbar.

Drill 6-14 Rapid Shooting

No. of players—Three per drill group

Explanation—Each A player has five balls at his feet. A players alternate shooting at the goal from outside the penalty area as seen in the diagram. As soon as the goalkeeper recovers from receiving one ball another player shoots his ball.

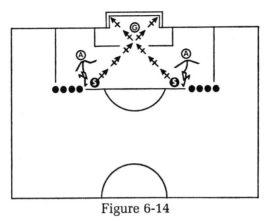

Figure 6-14

Drill 6-15 High Balls—Low Balls

No. of players—Three per drill group

Explanation—A serves low balls and B serves high balls alterna-
tively at the goalkeeper. Balls are hand served in rapid succession.

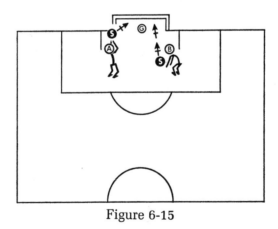

Figure 6-15

Drill 6-16 Alert

No. of players—Six or more plus one goalkeeper

Explanation—The players outside the penalty area pass a ball among
themselves. Without warning, one of the players takes a shot at the
goal.

Purpose—Goalkeepers practice following the ball as it moves across
the face of the goal.

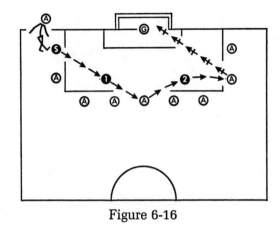

Figure 6-16

Drill 6-17 Catch, Return, Dive

No. of players—Two per drill group

Explanation—A ball is served to the far post to the goalkeeper who is lying on the ground with his hands on another ball. The goalkeeper quickly gets to his feet and catches, or dives and catches, the thrown ball. When he gets possession, he immediately throws the ball back to the server and dives to get his hands on the ball near the other post. Repeat this same procedure.

Purpose—This is a drill to improve the goalkeepers quickness and agility.

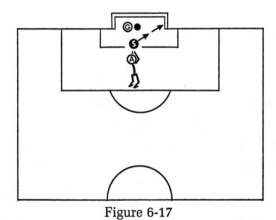

Figure 6-17

Drill 6-18 Side Roll and Dive (No Diagram)

No. of players—Two per drill group

Explanation—Balls are served toward the goalkeeper in the following manner: The goalkeeper performs a side shoulder roll. As soon as the goalkeeper regains his feet, another ball is thrown. If the goalkeeper shoulder rolls to the right the ball should be thrown to the right. If he rolls to the left, the ball should be thrown to the left. Balls are thrown just out of the goalkeepers reach so that he needs to dive in order to catch the ball. He is not allowed to take a step before he dives.

Purpose—This is an agility, pressure drill.

FUNCTIONAL DRILLS

Drill 6-19 Quick Recovery

No. of players—Five per drill group

Explanation—Cones or flags are placed at random inside the goal area. A, B, C, and D are assigned numbers. They dribble around inside the penalty area, but outside the goal area. The coach calls out a number and the player assigned to that number raises his hand for the goalkeeper to adjust his position. The number of the player called shoots quickly at the goal with the side of his foot. The player should attempt to hit one of the many flags or cones that are placed in front of the goal before the ball goes in the goal.

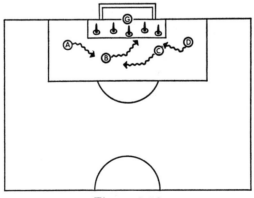

Figure 6-19

Purpose—Goalkeepers practice adjusting their positions and gathering balls that have rebounded off the flags or cones.

Drill 6-20 Distract the Goalkeeper

No. of players—Four per drill group

Explanation—C shoots balls at the goal. A and B distract the goalkeeper by faking a kick at the ball or by running in front of the balls kicked by player C. A and B are not permitted to touch the ball.

Purpose—Goalkeepers practice catching balls in a game-like atmosphere.

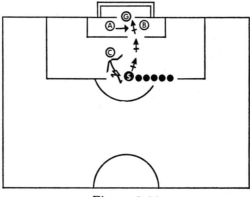

Figure 6-20

Drill 6-21 Target Throwing

No. of players—Two per drill group

Explanation—A cone is placed approximately twenty yards outside the penalty area, as seen in the diagram. A kicks balls at the goal. As soon as the goalkeeper receives the ball, B moves toward the goalkeeper in an attempt to prevent the goalkeeper from moving forward. The goalkeeper tries to throw the ball and to knock the cones down.

Purpose—Goalkeepers practice starting a quick counterattack and throwing toward a target under pressure.

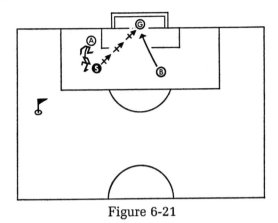

Figure 6-21

Drill 6-22 Cross and Shoot

No. of players—Four per drill group

Explanation—A passes to B, B dribbles, and either crosses or shoots the ball before he reaches the penalty area line. All shots are with the side of the foot on a "1-touch" basis. Passes and shots are only permitted outside the penalty area.

Purpose—Goalkeepers practice narrowing the angle and quickly adjusting their positions according to the position of the ball.

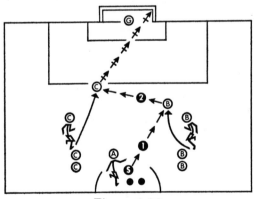

Figure 6-22

Drill 6-23 Recover and Narrow the Angle

No. of players—Seven per drill group

Explanation—A and B practice attacking the goal from a narrow angle. As soon as A completes or fails at his attack, B starts his attack around the cone. Then repeat the same procedure with the next player from the other side. Alternate attacks, first from the left, then from the right.

Purpose—Goalkeepers practice cutting the angle under pressure.

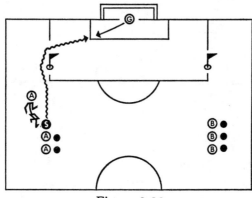

Figure 6-23

Drill 6-24 Coming Out

No. of players—Four per drill group

Explanation—A, B, and C are given different instructions about how to handle the shot at the goal. For example, tell A to shoot it past the goalkeeper when he comes out of the goal. Tell B to chip over the goalkeeper and tell C to dribble and try to beat the goalkeeper.

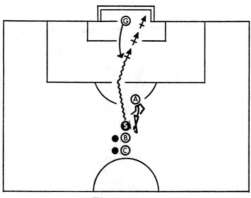

Figure 6-24

Purpose—Goalkeeper practices different approaches used to beat or pass him when he comes out of the goal.

Drill 6-25 Cut Off

No. of players—Six or more per drill group

Explanation—A and C alternate throwing balls high in the air to a position inside the goal area. The goalkeeper attempts to cut off these balls. As soon as the goalkeeper controls a ball another one is thrown from the other side of the eighteen-yard line. B's job is to disrupt the goalkeeper's attempts to cut off the balls but B is not allowed to touch the goalkeeper.

Purpose—Goalkeepers practice cutting off high balls coming from the wing area.

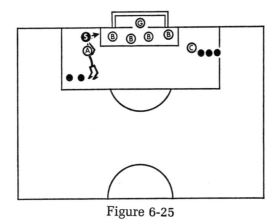

Figure 6-25

Drill 6-26 Dive and Cover Up

No. of players—Four per drill group

Explanation—Balls are thrown to either side of the goalkeeper by player A. Balls are thrown so that the goalkeeper must dive to control them. The goalkeeper dives, catches, and cuddles to protect the ball. If he bobbles the ball player B attempts to kick it out of his hands. This should be done carefully in a manner so as not to injure the goalkeeper. The goalkeeper is restricted to diving without taking a step.

Purpose—Goalkeepers practice catching and covering up balls that they have caught.

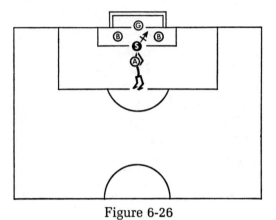

Figure 6-26

II

BASIC PATTERNS

Soccer Coaches are always talking about soccer being a game of time and space. What does this mean, and how can an individual player or a small group of players use time and space to their advantage? In broad terms, the defense wants to deny or limit time and space available to the attacking team. The attacking team wants to manipulate or trick the defenders into giving up precious time and space. How do you manipulate or trick the defense to give up time and space? This for the most part is done in small groups of one, two, three, and sometimes four players. Also, for the most part, this is accomplished when the players are near the ball. So far we have established "who" and "where" but the big question is: "how?" The "how" is accomplished by the following deceptive or diversionary tactics and by establishing numerical superiority in the area around the ball.

Wall passes—This is a maneuver in which you force defenders to play the ball, thus causing space to open up.

Back passes—This maneuver creates space and draws defenders out of position.

Crisscross runs—This maneuver forces defenders to decide which player to follow or to guard. It also creates numerical superiority, leading to open space.

Decoy runs—This maneuver is used to draw defenders away from a specific area of the field to create open space for a teammate to exploit.

Diagonal runs—This maneuver is used to cause defenders to position themselves in a straight line across the field, thus opening space behind them. It is also used to draw defenders from a specific area of the field and once again create open space.

Loop runs—This is a maneuver used to make the defenders think you are going in a certain direction. However, you quickly loop back and reverse the direction. This is another way of creating open space.

Exchanging positions—This is a maneuver during which attackers maintain depth and width while at the same time penetrating the defense. This maneuver forces defenders to decide which player to guard. When one defender is required to cover two areas at the same time, space is created for attackers to exploit.

Quick switching—This is a maneuver used to position the ball in another section of the field that is less crowded and where numerical superiority can be achieved in the attacking team's favor. Space is more plentiful in less crowded areas of the field.

Return passing—This maneuver causes the defenders to draw toward the ball, leaving space for the attacking team to exploit.

Blind side runs—In this maneuver, attackers run behind the defenders.

During match play, good players automatically recognize the opportunities to use and to execute the preceding diversionary tactics without hesitation. These players create their own opportunities and space, which create opportunities for teammates.

The first ten drills in the "Small Group Passing Drill" chapter are examples of the above diversionary tactics. First, these drills are learned without opponents, next with opponents applying limited pressure, and then against all out pressure. Eventually you should practice these movements in small-sided games. In a small-sided game, when one team is having difficulty in executing these tactics, you can reduce the number of players on the opposing team. This gives numerical superiority to the team having difficulty.

In small-sided games, a coach can stop play periodically to show players how to use diversionary tactics, especially when a player misses an opportunity to execute. At first a coach can have the player walk through the movement required for the tactic, and then have him run through it. As a coach sees his players executing these tactics correctly, he can recognize and congratulate them. He should encourage those who have executed well.

A coach may have his team play keep-away on one-half of the field with four or five on a side. During play, each time a diversionary tactic is executed, the player who initiated the tactic calls out the name of the tactic. For example: "Wall!" Before long players will not only know the names of these tactics but they will visualize and experience over and over how to set up these moves and how they can be carried out.

In this section you will find moving passing drills and small group passing drills. Moving passing drills are used to teach passing discipline, concentration, and support play. These are also used extensively early in a season. The small group passing drills in this chapter concentrate on small group tactical manuevers that are used to penetrate the opponent's defense.

7

Moving Passing

In order to move a soccer ball toward a goal, a certain amount of restraint must be evident among the players involved. At times the ball must be moved backward, sideward, diagonally, a completely across the field. It isn't just kicked straight ahead by every player who comes in contact with it, or possession would easily be lost. In soccer, the shortest distance from one point to another is not necessarily a straight line. Therefore, discipline, patience, and concentration along with skill and tactical awareness somehow need to be incorporated into the training process. These mental qualities and physical abilities are developed through participation in moving passing drills.

Rote technical skill is not enough. Players must not only possess the ability to perform skills, but also to perform them while moving.

These exercises develop teamwork and support play and reinforce trapping and passing skills. They should not be performed in a monotoned fashion. The rhythm and tempo should flow, yet it should not become predictable. Even though players are repeating exact patterns, the speed at which these patterns are performed should vary.

The principal ingredients of these drills are a combination of one or more of the following diversionary small group tactics.

1. return passing
2. overlapping
3. faking a pass to one player and passing to another
4. take-overs and fake take-overs
5. criss-cross patterns
6. exchanging positions
7. wall passing
8. give and go passing
9. letting a ball go through to another player

A drill illustrating each of the above tactics is included in this chapter. A coach could include one or two or more of these moves into a drill.

Ball control requires skill, patience, concentration, and discipline. Players in small groups can collectively acquire and improve these qualities and abilities through participation in moving passing drills.

Drill 7-1 Wall, Square, Square, Wall

No. of players—Two per drill group

Distance—A to B—10 to 15 yards

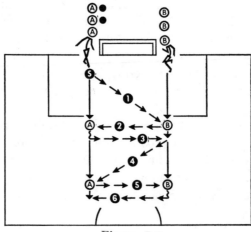

Figure 7-1

Explanation—A passes diagonally forward to B. B passes square to A. A square passes back to B. B then passes diagonally forward to player A.

Purpose—This is a moving passing drill that contains a wall pass and two square passes between the wall passes.

Drill 7-2 Two Man Moving Wall Pass

No. of players—Two per drill group

Distance—A to B—10 to 15 yards.

Explanation—A passes diagonally forward to player B. B square passes to A. A passes diagonally forward to B, etc.

Purpose—Two players practice wall passing on the move.

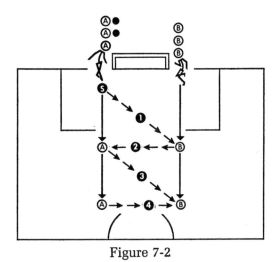

Figure 7-2

Drill 7-3 Step Over It

No. of players—Three per drill group

Distance—A to C—10 to 15 yards, C to B—10 to 15 yards

Explanation—A passes diagonally to C. C steps over the ball and lets it go on to B. B repeats the same procedure.

Purpose—Players practice a moving passing drill that includes passing, trapping, and a diversionary trick (stepping over the ball).

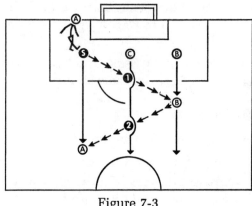

Figure 7-3

Drill 7-4 Take Over

No. of players—Three per drill group

Distance—A to B—10 to 15 yards, A to C—10 to 15 yards

Explanation—A dribbles diagonally. When he approaches B, he leaves the ball behind and B dribbles on toward C, and so on.

Purpose—Players practice dribbling and a diversionary trick (take-over).

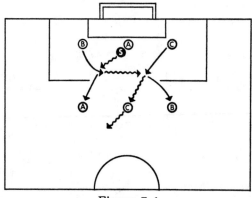

Figure 7-4

Drill 7-5 Fake and Pass

No. of players—Three per drill group

Distance—A to B—10 to 15 yards, A to C—10 to 15 yards

Explanation—A fakes a pass to C and passes diagonally to B. B square passes to A, and then A fakes a pass to B and passes diagonally to player C.

Purpose—Players practice a moving passing drill that includes passing, trapping and a diversionary trick (faking a pass to one player and passing to another player).

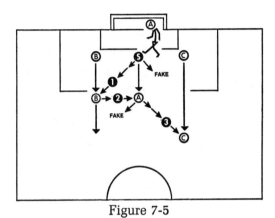

Figure 7-5

Drill 7-6 Overlapping

No. of players—Three per drill group

Distance—A to B—10 to 15 yards, A to C—10 to 15 yards

Explanation—A passes diagonally to player B and then A overlaps B. B dribbles to the center and passes off to C. B overlaps C and

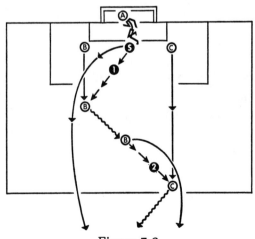

Figure 7-6

C dribbles to the center. The same procedure is continued until players reach the other end of the field.

Purpose—Players practice a moving passing drill that includes passing, dribbling, and a diversionary trick (overlapping).

Drill 7-7 Return Passing

No. of players—Three per drill group

Distance—A to B—10 to 15 yards, A to C—10 to 15 yards

Explanation—A passes diagonally forward to B. B passes diagonally back to A. A dribbles straight ahead and repeats the same procedure with player C.

Purpose—Players practice a moving passing drill that includes passing, trapping, and a diversionary trick (return passing).

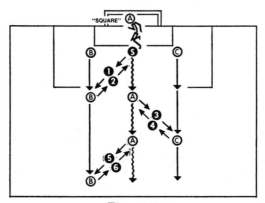

Figure 7-7

Drill 7-8 Wall and Step Over

No. of players—Three per drill group

Distance—A to B—10 to 15 yards, B to C—10 to 15 yards

Explanation—A passes diagonally forward to B, and then B passes diagonally forward to A. A sends a square pass to B but B steps over the ball letting it go on to player C. C repeats the same procedure.

Purpose—Players practice a moving passing drill that includes passing, trapping, and two diversionary tricks (wall pass and a step-over).

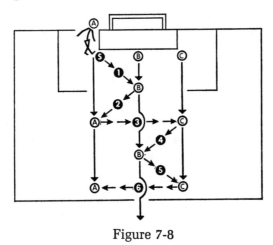

Figure 7-8

Drill 7-9 Up, Back, and Thru

No. of players—Three per drill group

Distance—A to B—10 to 15 yards, A to C—10 to 15 yards

Explanation—A passes straight ahead to player B. B passes diagonally back to C. C passes through to the overlapping A player. Repeat the same procedure to the other end of the field.

Purpose—Players practice a moving passing drill used to penetrate the defense.

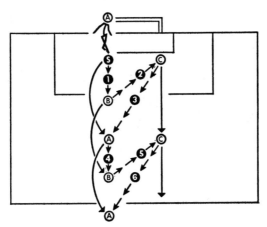

Figure 7-9

Drill 7-10 Three Man Criss-cross

No. of players—Three per drill group

Distance—A to B—10 yards, A to C—10 yards

Explanation—A passes diagonally forward in front of C. B runs over to receive A's pass. C runs across before B makes his move or run. B receives and controls the ball and then square passes back to A. On each pass by player A, player C makes a decoy run and B receives and controls the ball.

Purpose—Players practice a moving passing drill that includes passing, trapping, and two diversionary tricks (criss-cross runs and decoy runs).

Variation—The same drill, except players alternate receiving and making decoy runs. First, B receives A's pass and C decoys. Next, C receives the ball and B makes the decoy run.

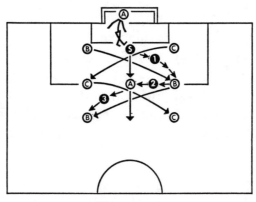

Figure 7-10

Drill 7-11 Dribble, Back Pass, Pass

No. of players—Three per drill group

Distance—A to B—10 yards, A to C—10 yards

Explanation—A dribbles diagonally forward and passes back to B. B passes diagonally forward to C. A takes B's original position and C, with the ball, is in A's original position. This procedure is repeated moving down the field.

Purpose—Players practice a moving passing drill involving passing, dribbling, and controlling a ball.

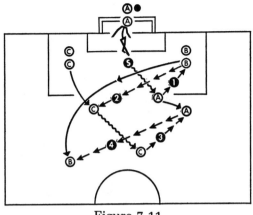

Figure 7-11

Drill 7-12 Pass, Dribble, Step on It

No. of players—Three per drill group

Distance—A to B—10 yards, A to C—10 yards

Explanation—A passes diagonally forward to B. B dribbles diagonally forward and steps on the ball and leaves it for C. C takes the ball and passes to A, thus repeating the cycle.

Purpose—Players practice a moving passing drill involving passing, dribbling, and controlling.

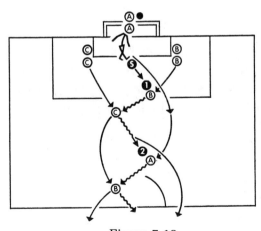

Figure 7-12

Drill 7-13 Three Man Dribble, Step On

No. of players—Three per drill group.

Distance—A to B—10 yards, A to C—10 yards

Explanation—A dribbles diagonally across in front of B. A steps on the ball and leaves it for B. B dribbles across in front of C and leaves the ball for C. This procedure is repeated as they progress down the field.

Purpose—Players practice a moving dribbling drill that includes a take-over.

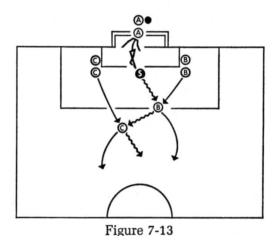

Figure 7-13

Drill 7-14 Exchange, Decoy, and Criss-cross

No. of players—Three per drill group

Distance—A to C—10 yards, C to B—10 yards

Explanation—A passes diagonally forward to B. B runs and collects the ball and dribbles diagonally forward. C makes a diagonal decoy run before B makes his run.

   B initiates the second phase of this drill. In this phase, B passes the ball, C receives the ball and dribbles diagonally forward, and player A makes a diagonal decoy run. This procedure is continued down the field.

Purpose—Players practice a moving passing drill that includes passing, trapping, and dribbling. Players practice exchanging positions, criss-cross runs, and decoy runs.

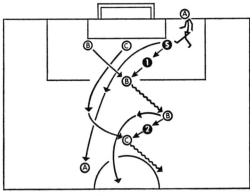

Figure 7-14

Drill 7-15 Three Man Give and Go

No. of players—Three per drill group

Distance—A to B—10 yards, A to C—10 yards

Explanation—B runs to a position straight ahead of A. A passes to B and B "1-touch" passes back to A. A chips the ball to C, who has moved to a position ten yards forward of B, as seen in the diagram

A overlaps and moves to the outside position, while B moves to the other outside position, and C is in the middle. This is the position where the second phase of the drill begins by C passing forward to A, etc.

Purpose—Players practice a moving passing drill that includes passing, trapping, and a diversionary trick (give and go).

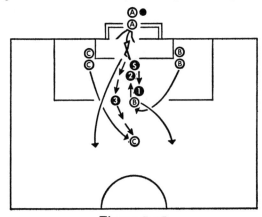

Figure 7-15

Drill 7-16 Overlap Fitness

No. of players—Three per drill group

Distance—A to B—10 to 15 yards, A to C—10 to 15 yards

Explanation—A passes to B and A overlaps B. B passes to C and B overlaps C. C passes to A and so on. When they get near the other end of the field, the ball is passed to player A in Group II and the same procedure is performed going in the other direction by Group II. Group II passes to Group III, etc.

Purpose—Players practice an overlaping moving passing drill and at the same time improve their physical fitness.

Figure 7-16

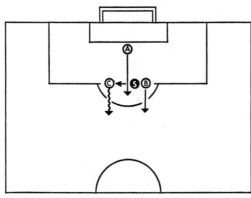

Figure 7-17

Drill 7-17 Commander

No. of players—Three per drill group

Distance—A, B, and C form a fifteen-yard triangle.

Explanation—A, the rear player, is the commander and gives instructions to B and C while all three players are moving down the field. A uses commands like "Back", "Square", "Thru", etc.

Purpose—Players practice communicating with each other.

Variation—Players perform the same drill against one defender.

Drill 7-18 1, 2, 3, Cross and Support

No. of players—Three per drill group

Distance—A to B—10 yards, B to C—30 to 40 yards

Explanation—A passes to B and B passes back to A. A then passes back to B and immediately runs across the field to support player C. B crosses the ball to C. Repeat the same procedure on the other side of the field.

Purpose—Players practice a quick switching and supporting maneuver while moving down the field.

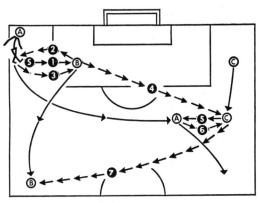

Figure 7-18

Drill 7-19 Five Man Overlap

No. of players—Five per drill group

Distance—10 yards between players.

Explanation—A passes to B and A overlaps B. B passes to C and overlaps C. C passes to D and C overlaps D. D passes to E and D overlaps E, and so on down the field. Each player has the responsibility to be in a position to receive the ball. Walk players through this drill and, as learning takes place, pick up the pace.

Purpose—Players practice overlapping and supporting the player with the ball.

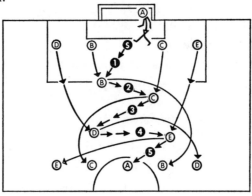

Figure 7-19

Drill 7-20 Half-Field Triangle Pass

No. of players—Twelve per drill group

Explanation—A dribbles and passes to B. B runs toward A to receive the pass. B drops the ball off for A and B sprints to receive a return pass from A. B dribbles and passes to C, etc.

Purpose—This is a moving passing drill involving a variety of passing distances—medium, short, and long passes.

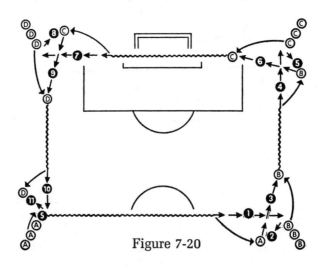

Figure 7-20

8

Small Group Passing

The main objective of small group passing drills is to penetrate the defense so that the ball can be moved in to a position for a shot at the goal. Before the small group passing drills can be effective, however, the players must be able to display a reasonable quality and quantity of technical skills. Yet a coach should not wait until skills are perfected before introducing players to small group maneuvers. Skills and techniques should be perfected and honed in a tactical setting. In this way, the technique is more meaningful and relates to its use in a game.

During practice sessions, these drills help players to develop a secret language. They learn to communicate among each other without saying a word. For example, a rear player passes forward to another teammate, after he passes he sprints forward to receive a return wall pass. How did the first player receiving the pass know to return the pass? Through the drill process, he experienced and developed habits that enabled him to carry out this task automatically. It may have been the way he accelerated after he passed the ball, it may have been the look in his eyes, or it may have been the way he passed the ball that clued his teammate in to what he wanted him to do. But whatever it was, both players understood each other's intentions without a spoken word. This type of understanding among players allows the game to flow and at the same time achieve penetration.

As your opponent's behavior is not always predictable, players should be prepared to cope with any inconsistencies. They should be given alternatives for this unexpected behavior. For instance, during the execution of a wall pass, an opponent could quickly position himself to prevent the return pass. Preparing players to meet this new twist is just as important as teaching them how to execute a wall pass. Knowing when to keep the ball and dribble off in a different direction is as much a part of the preparation of players as is the action of the original intent of the drill, which was to make a successful wall pass.

Through practicing small group drills and alternatives within small group drills, players can develop the expertise to execute quickly and effectively. These drills will give your players the confidence to handle and win a greater number of encounters.

The first sixteen passing drills in this chapter are drills for two players while the last eleven are for three players. Combinations with more than three players tend to break down during execution. Therefore, for the sake of simplicity, these drills were not included in this book.

A METHOD FOR SMALL GROUP PASSING SESSIONS

Very few coaches set time aside for players to practice on their own, which is a mistake for a number of reasons. First, they, the players, never get a chance to think for themselves about what they are doing right or what they are doing wrong in a game. Second, their initiative and creativity are not being developed by a coach who directs every phase of a practice session. Third, in an informal, relaxed atmosphere, players in small groups can concentrate better than a group that is being told every minute what to do.

This type of training is most effective after the season has gotten underway. The coaches responsibility is to make the small groups aware of problem areas such as lack of concentration, and dead ball situations that fell apart in previous games. A coach then sends small groups of players (three or four) to a separate section of the field to work on a phase of the game that needs attention. He, the coach, should not interfere unless players are wasting time, request his assistance, or perform in a manner that is unproductive in terms of soccer common sense.

Each player in the small group should have a chance to set up or to re-create an actual game situation that he feels he needs to work on and perfect. Cooperation of all players in the small groups is necessary for this to be effective. Furthermore, each player should be given the opportunity for the repetition that is needed for learning to occur.

It is obvious that players need to have reached a certain level of maturity to make this method of training productive. You will be surprised how conscientious players are about this training method.

Drill 8-1 Wall

No. of players—Two per drill group

Distance—A to B—10 to 15 yards apart, A to the cone—15 yards.

Explanation—A passes to B. A runs around the cone and B passes back to A with a "1-touch" pass. A gets in B's line and B gets in A's line.

Purpose—Players practice wall passing. This is a common way of getting behind defenders when two players are facing a defender.

Variation—A fakes a wall pass and dribbles around the cone and toward the goal.

Variation—A passes to B. B fakes passing back to A and turns and dribbles toward the goal for a shot.

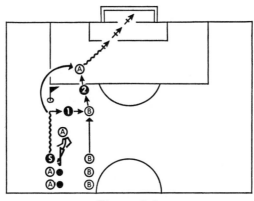

Figure 8-1

Drill 8-2 Scissors

No. of players—Two per drill group.

Distance—A to B—10 to 15 yards, A and B to the cone—10 to 15 yards

Explanation—A dribbles close to the front of the cone. A leaves the ball and B quickly picks it up and dribbles by the cone. B passes back to A. A gets in B's line and A gets in back of B's line.

Purpose—A scissors pass is used to force a defender to make a choice as to which attacker he should guard.

Variation—A keeps the ball and continues to dribble toward the goal and then passes to B.

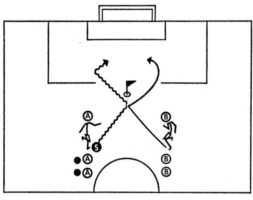

Figure 8-2

Drill 8-3 Give and Go

No. of players—Two per drill group

Distance—A to B—15 yards

Explanation—B runs forward to receive a pass from A. B "1-touches" the pass back to A. B breaks toward the goal and A sends an appropriate pass or chip to B. A gets in B's line and B gets in A's line.

Purpose—Players practice a give and go pass. This is used when players are lined up one ahead of the other.

Variation—B fakes a pass to A and B dribbles off.

Variation—B passes back to A and then decoys the opponent to one side while A dribbles toward the goal.

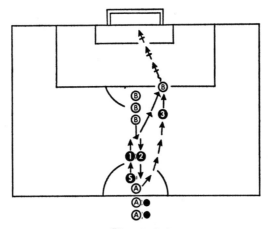

Figure 8-3

Drill 8-4 Wall, Square Pass

No. of players—Two per drill group

Distance—A and B are twenty yards apart.

Explanation—A dribbles a few times and passes to B who is dropping back toward A to receive the ball. B "1-touch" square passes to A. A dribbles toward the goal and either passes off to B or keeps the ball. This depends on what the situation dictates. A gets in B's line and B gets in A's line.

Purpose—This is a variation of a wall pass using a square pass to get into the space behind the defender.

Variation—B fakes passing back to A and dribbles off in the other direction.

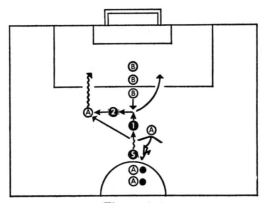

Figure 8-4

Drill 8-5 Pick Up and Over the Head

No. of players—Two per drill group

Distance—A to B—30 yards

Explanation—A passes to B and B lifts the ball up with his toe and flicks it over his head. Immediately after passing to B, A sprints to receive the over-the-head pass from B. A gets in B's line and B gets in A's line.

Variation—B fakes an over-the-head pass and dribbles to the opposite direction from which A has gone.

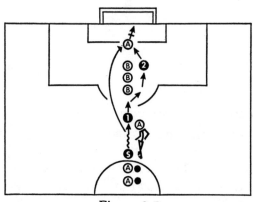

Figure 8-5

Drill 8-6 Overlap and Fake Overlap

No. of players—Two per drill group

Distance—A to B—30 yards

Explanation—A dribbles forward while B drops back. A square passes to B and then overlaps B and receives a pass from B. A dribbles or passes back to B depending on whatever the situation dictates.

Purpose—This is a two-man maneuver used to get into the space behind the defender.

Variation—Fake Overlap—A passes to B and overlaps B. B fakes a pass to A who is overlaping from right to left. B keeps the ball, turns, and dribbles off to his right.

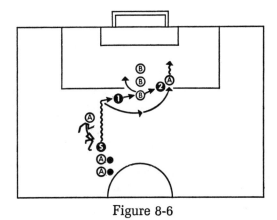

Figure 8-6

Drill 8-7 Criss-cross and Back Heel

No. of players—Two per drill group

Distance—A to B—10 to 15 yards

Explanation—A passes forward. B runs to gather the ball. A criss-crosses around behind B's back to receive a return pass from B if the situation dictates such a pass. A gets into B's line and B gets in A's line.

Purpose—Players practice a two-man combination to get into the space behind a defender.

Variation—A delays his run and B sprints to the ball and heels it immediately back to A.

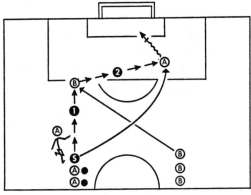

Figure 8-7

Drill 8-8 Blind Side Run

No. of players—Two per drill group

Explanation—B runs across the field behind the cone and receives a pass from A. A cuts behind the cone and toward the goal. A receives a return pass from B. A gets in B's line and B gets in A's line.

Purpose—This is a two-man maneuver used to get into the space behind defenders.

Variation—B calls for the ball but A keeps it, fakes a pass to B, and A then dribbles behind B and toward the goal.

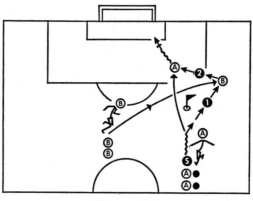

Figure 8-8

Drill 8-9 Veer Run

No. of players—Two per drill group

Distance—A to B—20 to 30 yards

Explanation—A passes to B who drops back to receive it. B "1-touch" passes back to A. B makes a veer run as seen in the diagram and then breaks to the goal to receive a "1-touch" pass or a chip from A. A gets in back of B's line and B gets in the back of A's line.

Purpose—This is a manuever used to create open space.

Variation—A keeps the ball and dribbles down the wing and then passes off to B as the situation dictates.

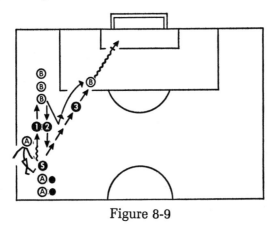

Figure 8-9

Drill 8-10 Dribble and Go Behind

No. of players—Two per drill group

Distance—A to B—15 to 20 yards

Explanation—A dribbles diagonally while B cuts behind A. A then passes to B.

Purpose—This is a means of penetrating open space behind a defender. The maneuver forces a defender to make a choice as to whom he must guard.

Variation—A keeps the ball and dribbles toward the goal.

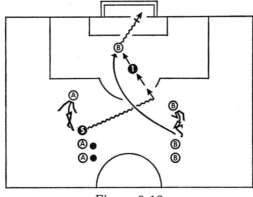

Figure 8-10

Drill 8-11 Space by Dribbling

No. of players—Two per drill group.

Distance—A to B—15 to 20 yards

Explanation—A passes to B and remains in his position. B dribbles diagonally past A. When B dribbles past A, he back heels the ball and A controls it and heads for the goal. B then runs to support A.

Purpose—B creates space by dribbling.

Variation—B keeps the ball and dribbles toward the goal. A follows for support.

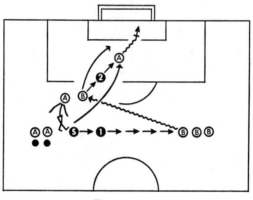

Figure 8-11

Drill 8-12 Change-of-Pace to Create Space

No. of players—Two per drill group

Distance—Cones are 10 yards apart, A to B —30 yards, A to the cones —15 yards, B to the cones —15 yards.

Explanation—B runs slowly across the field until he reaches the cones and then he sprints through the cones. A passes to the right side of player B. A gets into B's line and B gets in A's line.

Purpose—Players create space by a change-of-pace run.

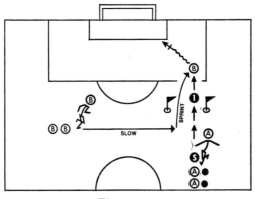

Figure 8-12

Drill 8-13 Step on It or Keep It

No. of players—Two per drill group

Distance—A to B —10 to 15 yards

Explanation—A dribbles toward B. As A dribbles in front of the cone he steps on the ball. B carries it past the cone and dribbles toward the goal while A moves into a support position. A gets in back of B's line and B gets into A's line.

Purpose—Players perform a quick switch to force the defender to make a choice as to which player to guard.

Variation—A keeps the ball and cuts toward the goal.

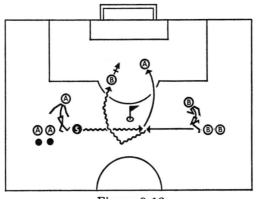

Figure 8-13

Drill 8-14 Loop Back

No. of players—Two per drill group

Distance—A to B—15 to 20 yards

Explanation—A dribbles slowly forward. B makes a diagonal run and quickly loops back. A sends a through pass to B's right side. A moves to a position for support or for a return pass.

Purpose—B makes a loop run to open space for a through pass.

Variation—A dribbles to his left if the defender follows player B.

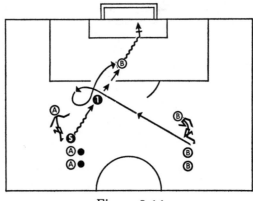

Figure 8-14

Drill 8-15 Diagonal Dribble Away

No. of players—Two per drill group

Distance—A to B—25 to 30 yards

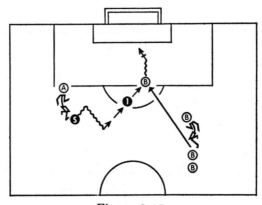

Figure 8-15

Explanation—A dribbles diagonally away from the goal. B makes a diagonal run to receive a pass toward the goal from A. A then moves to support B. A gets into B's line and B gets into A's line.

Purpose—B dribbles diagonally away from the goal to draw defenders out of position, thus opening space for a penetrating pass.

Drill 8-16 Changing the Angle

No. of players—Two per drill group

Distance—A to B—10 to 15 yards

Explanation—A passes to B. A moves square to receive a pass back from B. B breaks for the goal and A passes back to B.

Purpose—A moves to a position to make a thru pass to B.

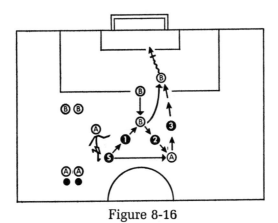

Figure 8-16

Drill 8-17 Dribble Decoy

No. of players—Three per drill group

Distance—A to B—10 to 15 yards, B to C—20 to 25 yards

Explanation—A passes to B. B dribbles square across the field and passes back to A. C comes from behind to receive a pass from A. B moves forward to support C.

Purpose—This is a combination pattern used to create space by dribbling and by use of a back pass.

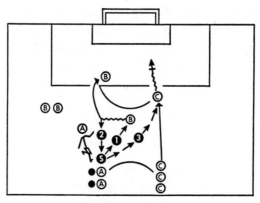

Figure 8-17

Drill 8-18 Three Man Overlap

No. of players—Three per drill group

Distance—A to B—10 yards, B to C—10 yards

Explanation—A passes diagonally to B and B passes diagonally to C. A runs behind B to receive a pass from C.

Purpose—A performs an overlap run to create space.

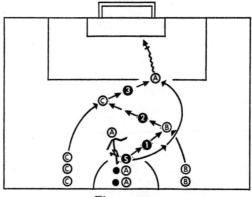

Figure 8-18

Drill 8-19 In, Back, Thru

No. of players—Three per drill group

Distance—A to B—15 yards, B to C—15 yards

Explanation—A passes diagonally forward to B. B passes diagonally back to C while A makes a run behind B to receive a pass from C.

Purpose—A back pass and an overlap run are performed to create open space.

Variation—The same drill except start the ball in position C.

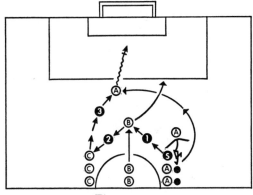

Figure 8-19

Drill 8-20 Overlap Down the Wing

No. of players—Three per drill group

Distance—A to B—10 to 15 yards, B to C—10 to 15 yards

Explanation—A passes diagonally to B. B passes square to player C. C passes diagonally to A.

Purpose—This is a combination pass used to move the ball down the wing using an overlap.

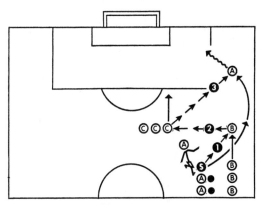

Figure 8-20

Drill 8-21 Blind-Side Down the Wing

No. of players—Three per drill group

Distance—A to B—15 yards, A to C—15 yards

Explanation—A passes to the space ahead of B. B passes straight ahead to the open space for C.

Purpose—This is a combination pass used to get the ball in the open space in the wing area by using a blind-side run.

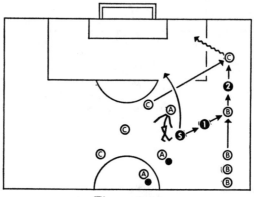

Figure 8-21

Drill 8-22 Veer and Criss-cross

No. of players—Three per drill group

Distance—A to C and B—15 yards

Explanation—B and C make veer runs then they execute a criss-cross run. A then passes to either player.

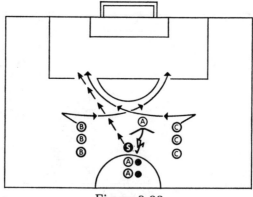

Figure 8-22

Purpose—This is a combination pass pattern to create space by using a back pass, a veer run, and a criss-cross run to free players to receive a penetrating pass.

Drill 8-23 Diagonal, Square, Back, Thru

No. of players—Three per drill group

Distance—A, B, and C form a fifteen-yard triangle.

Explanation—A passes diagonally to B. B square passes to C. C back passes to A and then B and C make a criss-cross run.

Purpose—This is a combination used to free players to receive a ball by using a criss-cross run.

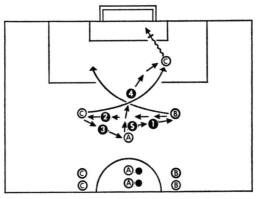

Figure 8-23

Drill 8-24 Outside Defender Overlap

No. of players—Three per drill group.

Distance—G, the goalkeeper, to A—20 yards, A to B—30 to 40 yards, C to B—30 to 40 yards

Explanation—The goalkeeper passes to the outside defender, A. The outside defender (A) passes to B who drops back to receive the pass. B gives a "1-touch" pass to C, the mid-field player. C sends a pass down the wing to player A, the overlapping fullback.

Purpose—This is a combination passing maneuver to get the ball to the overlapping outside defender.

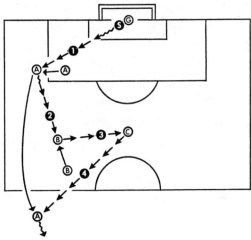

Figure 8-24

Drill 8-25 Decoy and a Delayed Run

No. of players—Three per drill group

Distance—A to B—15 yards, B to C—5 yards

Explanation—A dribbles to the eighteen-yard line and at the same time C performs a decoy run to open space for B to receive a pass. B delays his run to give C time to clear the space.

Purpose—This is a simple combination play used to open space by using a decoy.

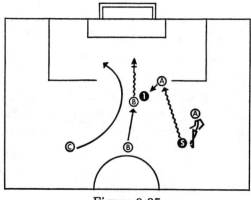

Figure 8-25

Drill 8-26 Mid-Field Cross

No. of players—Three per drill group

Distance—A to B—15 yards, B to C—10 to 15 yards

Explanation—A passes to B and then B "1-touch" passes back to A. B immediately runs diagonally toward the middle of the field. C runs behind B to receive a pass down the wing.

Purpose—This is a combination play used to open space by a back pass and a decoy run.

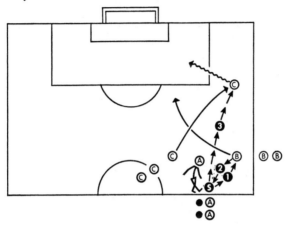

Figure 8-26

Drill 8-27 Target Man

No. of players—Three per drill group

Distance—See the diagram.

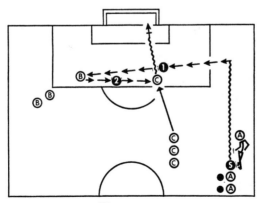

Figure 8-27

Explanation—A dribbles down the wing and sends a long pass to B. B heads or "1-touch" passes off to C. C must delay his run so he will meet the ball on the run.

Purpose—This is a combination involving a cross, a quick change of direction, and a delayed run used to penetrate the defense.

III

SPECIAL SITUATIONS

Periodic interruptions in a game occur because a ball goes out of bounds, goes over the end line, time runs out in a period, or a rule is broken. These situations are called dead ball situations or special situations. During these interruptions, players on the attacking team have time to organize and set up a maneuver or a set play to exploit their opponents. How well a team handles these situations can have a bearing on the outcome of a game.

It is a proven fact that many goals are scored from the maneuvers carried out in these special situations. A coach has the responsibility to prepare his players in practice sessions to take advantage of these opportunities, both offensively and defensively.

The following are special situations for which practice time should be set aside to improve and refine technique. Special situations are usually classified under the following categories:

1. penalty kick
2. free kick (direct and indirect)
3. corner kick
4. throw in
5. drop-ball
6. kick off

Of these special situations, penalty kicks, free kicks, and corner kicks are more likely to produce a goal than the others. For the sake of practicality, time assigned in a practice session to meet the challenge of special situations should relate to the chance that these situations can produce a score. In other words, more time should be assigned to practicing the first three special situations.

Many teams, in handling kick-off situations, merely push the ball forward its circumference then kick it back into their own half of the field so that the strikers can get enough time to penetrate the other half of the field. For this reason, kick-off set plays were not included in this book.

Dropped ball situations were also left out of this chapter, because merely gaining control is the objective of this special situation. Tactics used in special situations are similar to the tactics used in a regular game. The only difference is that the situation is started without pressure, giving the attacking team time to set up a preconceived plan to trick or deceive the opponents. The deceptive plans include decoy runs, quick surprises, or use of special talent. For example: a player can curve a ball around a wall and perform echelon runs and other deceptive and direct tactics. Players should be prepared to improvise when these situations do not work out the way they were planned.

9

Corner Crossing
and Corner Kicks

Defenders prefer to keep attackers out of the middle of the attack area of the field. In doing this, they must concede space in the outside wing area. For this reason, attackers use this less congested area to launch an attack on the goal.

Balls kicked from the corner area are aimed for three areas: near post, mid-goal area, and the far post. Regardless of the target area, players should not be standing and waiting for a crossed ball. They should time their runs from outside the area so they arrive in the target area when the ball arrives. They should also arrive with speed.

When crossing a ball, the position of the goalkeeper dictates the target area. If the goalkeeper is near the far post, the ball is sent to the near post area and likewise, if the goalkeeper is close to the near post, the ball is sent to the far post. In general, in far post crosses and near post crosses, the ball should land six or seven yards away from the goal. In any case, it should be far enough away from the goal so it will be risky for the goalkeeper to come out to catch it.

Depending on the position of the goalkeeper and the defenders, the attacker receiving the ball can deflect it across the face of the goal, deflect it back, or shoot straight at the goal. When it is deflected, players from the rear come forward for a shot on goal.

When heading the ball at the goal, the head should be well over the ball so the ball is headed in a downward direction.

It is a common practice to cross the ball to the mid-goal area. To clear this area of defenders, two attackers can decoy if one moves outward to the near post and the other decoys outward to the far post. In the space that is created, a third attacker moves in for a shot at the goal.

Frequently coaches discuss the controversy about whether to use the inswinger or the outswinger to cross a ball. Rather than look at it from the standpoint of which is best, we should consider the advantages of each of these two methods of crossing the ball.

The inswinger is sometimes used when attackers are going with the direction of a strong wind. In this case, a slight touch or a flick off the head of a teammate can cause the ball to end up in the goal. Furthermore, the wind itself could carry the ball into the goal. Also, when a goalkeeper has a reputation of staying back in the goal, an inswinger should be used.

The outswinger is extensively used because it curves in a path toward the receiving attacker. This enables attackers to impart more power to a scoring attempt. The goalkeeper is also less likely to come out and chase a ball that is curving away from him. Another advantage of the outswinger is that it enables the attacker to maintain a full view of the defenders and the goalkeeper while approaching the ball.

In any case, the inswinger or the outswinger should be placed so that it will be a gamble for the goalkeeper to attempt to cut it off.

The similarity of corner crossing and corner kicks is such that these two categories were placed in the same chapter. The main difference between the two is that in corner crossings, an opponent can put pressure on the kicker, whereas in corner kicks, the opponent must stay ten yards away from the kicker. Also, corner kicks cause players to be more aware of precisely when the ball will be kicked. Finally, the no offsides rule on corner kicks makes it easier for the attackers to get closer to the goal to receive the ball.

In defending against corner kicks, players have more time to establish defensive positions. The goalkeeper should stand near the far third or near the middle of the goalpost.

One defender should guard the far post and one defender should be in a position ten yards away from the kicker to prevent low kicks to the near post and also to put pressure on the kicker.

Other players are strategically placed throughout the goal and the penalty area or they play a strict man-for-man coverage.

Frequently, short corner kicks are used to draw defenders toward the ball. When the defenders are drawn out, the ball is quickly played behind them and another player then moves in for a shot at the goal.

Many goals are scored from the corner area. Therefore, the time spent on preparing players for corner kicks is time well spent. This will enable players to take maximum advantage of these situations when they occur in a game.

Drill 9-1 Two Man Overlap and Cross

No. of players—Two per drill group

Explanation—A passes to B. A overlaps B. B passes to A. B overlaps A, etc. The overlapping continues until players reach the corner area. At this point, the player in possession of the ball yells "Go." The player not in possession makes a curved run to the edge of the eighteen-yard line in the direction of the near post. The ball is crossed to the near post area for a shot on the goal.

Purpose—Players practice overlapping to get the ball down the wing area for a cross to the near post.

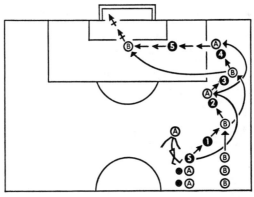

Figure 9-1

Drill 9-2 Dual Pass Cross

No. of players—Two per drill group

Explanation—On a signal (whistle), A and B, each with a ball, dribble to the corner of the eighteen-yard line. When they reach the corner, each passes his ball across the penalty area as seen in the diagram. A then shoots B's ball and B shoots A's ball.

Purpose—Players practice crossing and shooting crossed balls.

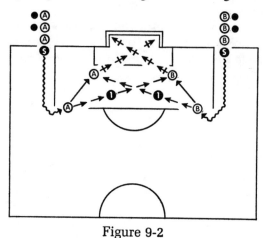

Figure 9-2

Drill 9-3 Three Man Overlap Wing Attack

No. of players—Three per drill group.

Distance—A to B—10 to 15 yards, A to C—10 to 15 yards

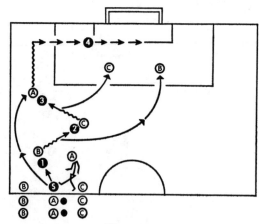

Figure 9-3

Explanation—A passes diagonally forward to B. A overlaps B. B dribbles and passes diagonally forward to C. B makes a run for the far post. C dribbles diagonally forward and passes to A. C makes a run to the near post. A dribbles down the wing and crosses to C or B.

Purpose—Players practice an overlap maneuver to get the ball down into the wing area.

Drill 9-4 Dribble to the Baseline and Cross

No. of players—Three per drill group

Distance—A to B—15 to 20 yards

Explanation—A dribbles to the baseline and crosses. B makes a loop run to improve his angle for a shot at the goal and to improve his timing, enabling him to arrive with speed.

Purpose—This is a crossing combination pattern that includes dribbling, passing, and shooting.

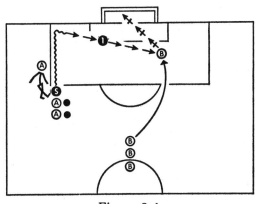

Figure 9-4

Drill 9-5 Down the Line

No. of players—Four per drill group

Distance—A to B—10 to 15 yards, A to C—25 to 35 yards

Explanation—Play starts on a signal (whistle), A passes in the corner to B and B "1-touch" passes it back to A. A passes it across the goal area to C. C must delay his run so he can meet the ball on the run. The defender enters the play when B touches the ball.

Purpose—Players practice passing, controlling, and shooting. This is a combination pattern originating from the corner area.

Rotation order—A to B, B to C, C to A.

Figure 9-5

Drill 9-6 One-on-two Cross Drill

No. of players—Four per drill group

Explanation—On a whistle, A dribbles down the sideline and tries to get close to the baseline to cross the ball. The defender's starting position is behind A and he keeps pressure on A. C makes a loop run so he arrives in the area of the crossed ball with speed.

Purpose—Players practice dribbling, feinting, and crossing a ball under pressure applied by a defender.

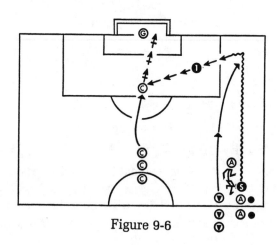

Figure 9-6

Drill 9-7 Pass Forward, Overlap and Cross

No. of Players—Four per drill group

Explanation—A passes to B and A overlaps B and receives a pass back from B. C times his run and shoots at the goal.

Purpose—Players practice an overlapping combination used to get the ball into position so it can be crossed.

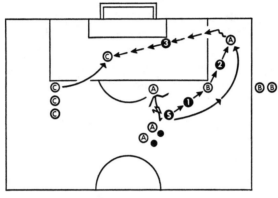

Figure 9-7

Drill 9-8 Back Pass and Criss-cross

No. of players—Four per drill group

Explanation—A passes to B, B "1-touch" passes it back to A. B and C make a criss-cross pattern. B makes his run first. A leads C with a long pass to the corner area. C crosses to B or D depending on which player is free to receive the pass.

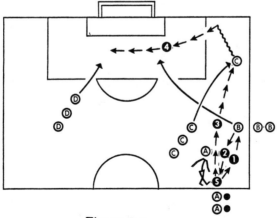

Figure 9-8

Purpose—B and C make criss-cross runs to get the ball down into the corner area so C can cross the ball to B to head it at the near post or D to head it at the far post.

Drill 9-9 Hurry

No. of players—Four per drill group

Explanation—A dribbles to the corner area and crosses the ball to B. B shoots at the goal. The defender puts pressure on A and B to move down the field quickly to get a clear shot at the goal. By moving the defender closer or further away from B, you can increase or decrease the pressure on player B to get his shot off quickly. B and the defender cannot move until A kicks the ball from the corner area.

Purpose—Player A practices crossing the ball from the corner area. Player B practices getting a shot off quickly.

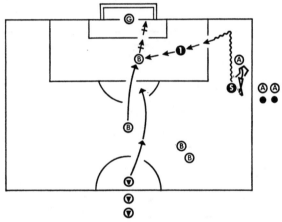

Figure 9-9

Drill 9-10 Back Pass—Near and Far Post Runs

No. of players—Five per drill group

Explanation—A passes to B and B passes at an angle back to A. A crosses the ball to either D, making a far post run, or C, running to the near post.

Purpose—Player B uses a back pass to enable A to get clear to cross the ball to D or C.

Variation—The same drill only D and C make criss-cross runs with D going to the near post and C going to the far post.

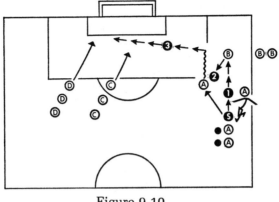

Figure 9-10

Drill 9-11 Cross and Wall Pass

No. of players—Five per drill group

Explanation—A serves a ball to player B. B controls the ball and tries to make a wall pass with either C player. The defender cannot move until player B touches the ball.

Purpose—Players practice a corner crossing maneuver and a wall pass to get a shot at the goal.

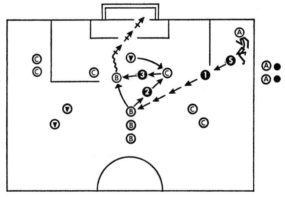

Figure 9-11

Drill 9-12 Three Man Timing

No. of players—Three per drill group

Explanation—A sends an inswinger into the penalty area. B runs and deflects the ball away from the goal. C comes up from the rear for a shot at the goal. C should time his run so that he arrives just at the right time.

Purpose—A deflected back pass is used so a player from the rear can take a shot at the goal.

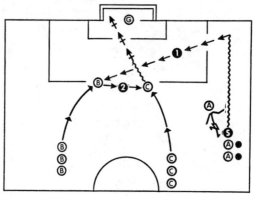

Figure 9-12

Drill 9-13 From the Rear

No. of Players—Three per drill group

Explanation—A sends an inward swinger pass into the penalty area. B runs and deflects the ball away from the goal. C comes from the rear for a shot at the goal. C should time his run so that he arrives at the right time.

Purpose—A deflected back pass is used so that a player from the rear can take a shot at the goal.

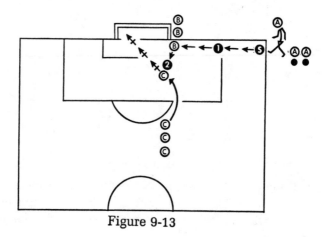

Figure 9-13

Drill 9-14 Step Over the Corner Kick

No. of players—Three per drill group

Explanation—A sends a ground pass toward the corner of the eighteen-yard line. C runs to the ball as if he will shoot it, but steps over the ball. B comes from the rear for a shot at the goal. Timing is important for this drill to be effective.

Purpose—This is a maneuver used to get the ball in the center of the field for a shot at the goal.

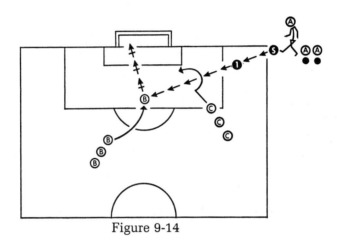

Figure 9-14

Drill 9-15 Near, Mid, Far Post Runs

No. of players—Seven per drill group

Distance—See the diagram.

Explanation—A crosses the ball. B, C, and D make runs at the goal as seen in the diagram. E and F back up and look for balls coming back out.

Purpose—Players B, C, and D practice a run designed to cover the near post, the middle area, and the far post area. E and F practice backing up the play.

Variation—Add defenders to increase the pressure of the drill and to make it more game-like.

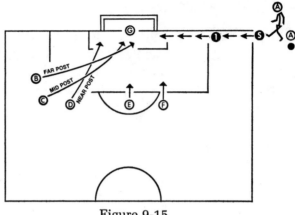

Figure 9-15

Drill 9-16 Short Corner

No. of players—Four per drill group

Explanation—B runs toward the corner. A passes to B. C runs forward to receive a pass from B and then C dribbles or shoots at the goal.

Purpose—This is a maneuver used when the defense does not station a man to play in the area near the kicker.

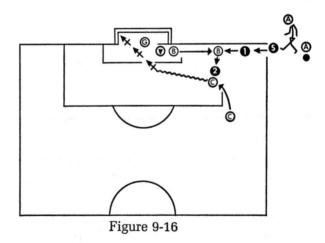

Figure 9-16

Drill 9-17 Long on the Ground Back Pass

No. of players—Four per drill group

Explanation—A sends a long corner kick on the ground as seen in the diagram. Just before the kick, C makes a decoy run out of this area. B comes from the rear for a shot at the goal.

Purpose—A long on the ground back pass and a decoy run are used to get a shot at the goal.

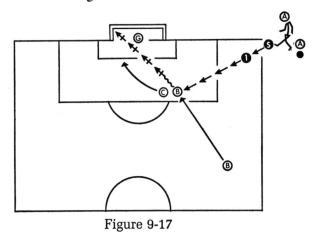

Figure 9-17

Drill 9-18 Head Back and Across

No. of players—Four per drill group

Explanation—A kicks the ball across the penalty area to B. B heads back to C and C shoots at the goal. C must delay his run for timing purposes.

Purpose—Players practice a corner kick that causes the ball to go across the face of the goal and then come back in the same direction to surprise the defenders.

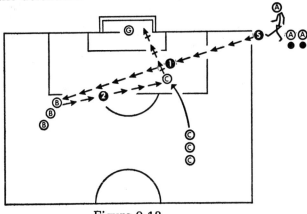

Figure 9-18

Drill 9-19 Corner Decoy

No. of players—Six per drill group.

Explanation—E, D, and C make decoy runs to draw defenders as seen in the diagram. A kicks the ball into the space created by E, D, and C. B comes from the rear for a shot on the goal.

Purpose—Players practice a corner kick that uses decoy runs to create space for another player to come from the rear for a shot at the goal.

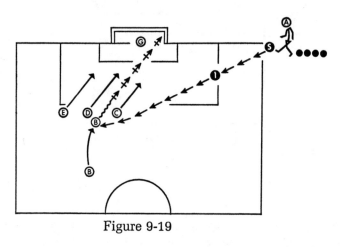

Figure 9-19

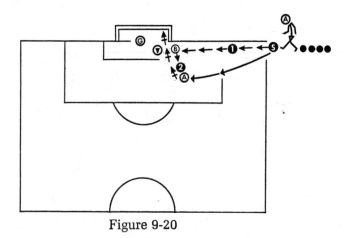

Figure 9-20

Drill 9-20 Head Back to the Kicker

No. of players—Three per drill group

Explanation—B runs across the goal area to receive the corner kick from A. Immediately after kicking the ball, A runs to receive a return pass or header from B. A then shoots at the goal.

Purpose—This is a corner kick maneuver used when opponents fail to cover the player taking the corner kick.

10

Throw-In

Intelligent soccer players are rarely caught napping when opponents try to execute a quick throw-in. A coach's responsibility is to condition his players to react immediately when a ball goes over the sidelines. Players should scurry to assume their defensive positions or to quickly assume their man to man marking.

Tight marking, especially in the area where the ball is being thrown, is a must. Also, special effort should be made to apply pressure on the player receiving the ball, for he is most vulnerable when he first makes contact with the ball.

When the ball is being thrown from a position close to the goal, players should protect the goal area as they would in a corner kick situation. Players should frequently be reminded that the near post is a target for an attacking player who can throw long distances. It is always wise to station your best headers in the near post area.

Conversely, in attacking, a throw-in can be an effective weapon to take advantage of a defending team that tends to relax and set up slowly. A frequent practice used to speed up a throw-in is to have the closest player to the ball, going out of bounds, take the throw-in. The teammates of the thrower must be alert to move into position to receive the quick throw-in, otherwise the effect will be lost.

Attacking players should spread out because it is easier to create space when players are not crowded into small area.

The ball should be thrown so that it can be easily controlled. The first choice is to throw the ball forward in the direction of the attack, but if this is not feasible, it can be thrown backward. Immediately after the throw, the thrower should move to support the player receiving the ball.

Tactical maneuvers used to free players from defenders are exchanging positions, criss-cross runs, decoy runs, change-of-pace runs, overlap runs, blind side runs, veer runs, and wall pass runs. The first eight drills in this chapter are examples of these types of tactical maneuvers.

The accuracy that can be achieved when throwing the ball makes it practical to use set plays to exploit opponents.

In the attack section of the field, a long accurate throw to the near post frequently results in a goal. Many times this particular throw-in is quickly deflected across the face of the goal and catches the goalkeeper by surprise.

If opponents show signs of poor physical fitness, quick throw-ins, especially in the beginning of the game, can wear them down. Then, in the latter stages of the game it will be difficult for the opponents to keep up with your team.

First practice the drills in this chapter without opponents. Once the team has mastered these drills, add opponents and other players to make each drill relate to an actual game situation.

Drill 10-1 Exchanging Positions

No. of players—Three per drill group

Explanation—C and B exchange positions, A thows to B. A should throw his pass so that B can receive it on the run.

Purpose— C and B exchange positions to enable B to become free to receive the throw-in.

Drill 10-2 Criss-cross Run

No. of players—Three per drill group

Explanation—C makes his run and B cuts behind C to receive the throw-in from A.

Purpose—Players B and C make criss-cross runs to free player B. A should lead B with his pass.

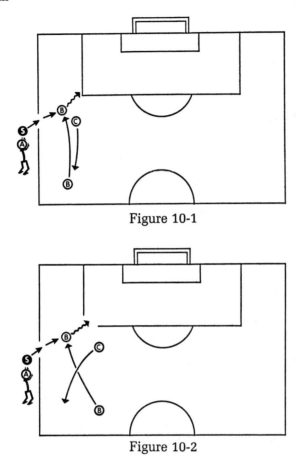

Figure 10-1

Figure 10-2

Drill 10-3 Overlap Throw-in

No. of players—Three per drill group

Explanation—B overlaps C to get free to receive a throw-in from player A.

Purpose—B overlaps C to get free to receive the throw-in.

Drill 10-4 Decoy and Run

No. of players—Two per drill group.

Explanation—C decoys to open space for B to receive the throw-in from player A.

Purpose—Player C makes a decoy run to get player B free to receive the throw in.

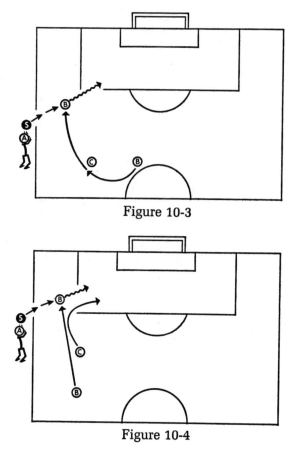

Figure 10-3

Figure 10-4

Drill 10-5 Veer Run

No. of players—Two per drill group

Explanation—B runs toward A and quickly changes direction and runs down the sideline to receive the throw-in from player A.

Purpose—Player B makes a veer run to free himself to receive the throw in.

Drill 10-6 Blind Side Run

No. of players—Four per drill group.

Explanation—B runs behind the defender to receive the throw in.

Purpose—B makes a blind side run to free himself to receive the throw-in from player A.

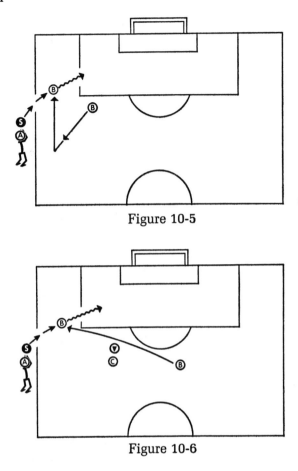

Figure 10-5

Figure 10-6

Drill 10-7 Change-of-pace Run

No. of players—Two per drill group

Explanation—B runs slowly for about ten yards and then quickly sprints to receive the throw-in. A should lead B so that he must run to catch up with the ball.

Purpose—B makes a change-of-pace run to free himself to receive the throw-in.

Drill 10-8 Throw-in Wall

No. of players—Three per drill group.

Explanation—A throws to B and B passes or heads the ball back to A. The pressure on player B is regulated by moving the defender closer or further away.

Purpose—This is a functional throw-in drill that allows the receiver to play the ball back to the thrower.

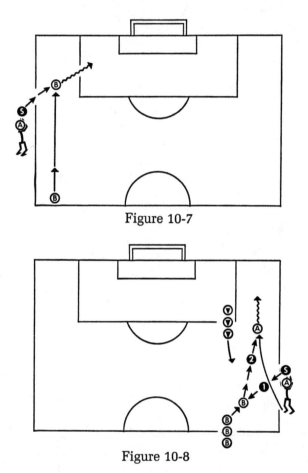

Figure 10-7

Figure 10-8

Drill 10-9 Three Man Blind Side Throw-in

No. of players—Three per drill group

Explanation—B runs toward A. A throws the ball to B's head. B heads the ball back to A. In the meantime, C makes his run behind B. A "1-touch" passes the ball for C to collect and advance with the ball down the field.

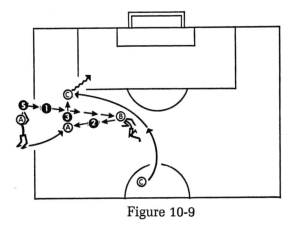

Figure 10-9

Purpose—This is a blind side maneuver used to keep control of the ball on a throw-in.

Drill 10-10 Four Man Throw-in Drill

No. of players—Four per drill group

Explanation—A throws the ball to the space in front of player **B**. B pushes the ball forward to player **C**. C passes to A. A sends the ball down the sideline to player **D**.

Purpose—This is a four-man combination maneuver to get the ball on the field.

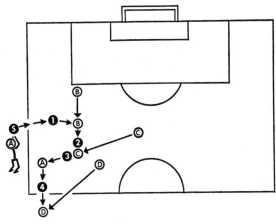

Figure 10-10

Drill 10-11 Quick Switch Throw-in

No. of players—Three per drill group

Explanation—A throws the ball away from the goal that he is attacking. B runs to the ball, controls it, and immediately crosses it to player C, who has made a run to the other side of the field.

Purpose—This is a quick switch maneuver. It is especially effective when opponents tend to congregate in the area where the throw is being taken.

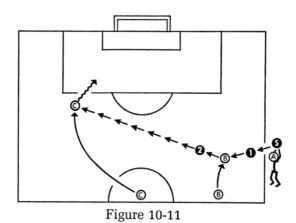

Figure 10-11

Drill 10-12 Quick Deflection

No. of players—Three per drill group

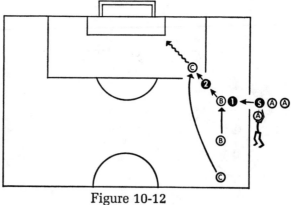

Figure 10-12

Explanation—A throws the ball in the air for B to deflect to player C.

Purpose—This is a simple deflection maneuver used to advance the ball.

Drill 10-13 Throw-in Timing Drill

No. of players—Four per drill group

Explanation—A throws the ball to the corner of the goal area line as seen in the diagram. B runs to the ball and deflects it across the face of the goal. C moves in and heads the ball at the goal. C must time his run so that he arrives with speed.

Alternate performing this drill with the players on the other side of the field.

Rotation order—A to C, B to A, C to B

Purpose—Players practice a long throw-in that is deflected across the goal for player C to come from the rear for a shot on the goal.

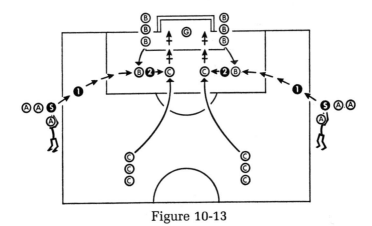

Figure 10-13

11

Direct and Indirect
Free Kicks

All players should be ready to take a free kick when the ball is not in position for a direct shot at the goal. Playing the ball quickly is especially effective against opponents who attend to argue about referee calls. Also, it is effective against teams that tend to relax when they hear a whistle blown. In these situations, and for the above reasons, the closest player to where the ball is awarded should quickly move to play the ball. Surprise, penetration, and maintaining possession are the three considerations when executing a free kick when a direct shot at the goal is not practical.

On the other hand, when a free kick is awarded within shooting range and a scoring chance, directly or indirectly, it should be taken by a player with good shooting ability. This player may also decide to play the ball quickly if the defense sets up slowly, or when the defense sets up incorrectly.

The player taking the shot should have an accurate, powerful shot and be able to curve the ball around a wall. Emotionally, he should be able to handle pressure situations in a calm, calculating manner. Other players with special talents and special abilities should be utilized in carrying out free kick situations. For example, station tall players and good headers in strategic positions.

When a free kick is awarded within shooting range, defending players should set up a wall as quickly as possible. In most cases, four or five players are sufficient to accomplish this. Less players are needed in the wall when the kick is awarded close to the sidelines or at a wide angle. One team member should be designated to set up the wall. He stands ten yards behind the ball to get a view of the situation. He positions the first player on the near post and then other players align themselves alongside this player. He further checks to see if the goalkeeper's view of the ball is obstructed. Some teams use the goalkeeper to set up the wall, but many coaches feel this is a poor choice.

A coach, in designing his own set plays to beat a wall, should arrange players so that opponents are drawn away from where the ball is intended to be played. For instance, an opponent positions himself in a gap alongside a wall where the ball is intended to be played. One attacking player should be assigned the responsibility of positioning himself so that the opponent who is in the gap must move out of the gap to guard him.

Many goals are scored from free kick situations. Players heighten their chances to meet the challenges of free kick situations if they are prepared both offensively and defensively in their practice sessions.

Drill 11-1 Running Across the Wall

No. of players—Two full teams

Explanation—As A is approaching the ball to kick it, C runs across

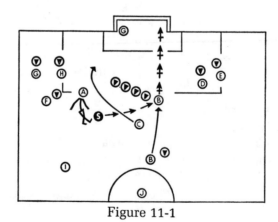
Figure 11-1

the face of the wall. A kicks the ball in the gap for B to come forward for a shot at the goal.

Purpose—This maneuver is used to make the defenders think the ball will be going to C when it is actually going to B who is coming up from the rear.

Drill 11-2 Fake Pick-up

No. of players—Two full teams

Explanation—A walks to the ball and pretends he is going to pick it up. Instead, he passes it to B, B "1-touch" passes ahead of C. C shoots at the goal. After A plays the ball to B, A runs toward the goal as seen in the diagram.

Purpose—This is a method of taking an indirect free kick. Defenders think the ball will be played one way and it is played the other direction.

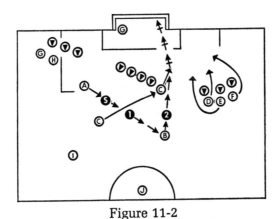

Figure 11-2

Drill 11-3 Let Thru

No. of players—Two full teams

Explanation—A passes to B. B lets it go through his legs or he back heels it to player C. C comes from the rear for the shot.

Purpose—This combination is used when the defenders on the end of the line tend to charge the ball.

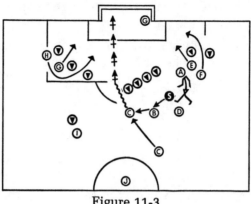

Figure 11-3

Drill 11-4 Blocking the View

No. of players—Two full teams

Explanation—Attacking players set up a wall in front of the defending team's wall. On a signal, the ball is chipped over the wall or through the gaps on either side of the wall. This depends on the way the opponents set up.

Purpose—This formation is used to obstruct the view of the ball from the defending team.

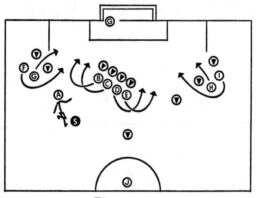

Figure 11-4

Drill 11-5 Draw

No. of players—Two full teams

Explanation—As soon as B starts his run, A pushes the ball forward. B makes a short veer run and "1-touch" passes the ball outside the wall. C comes from the rear for a shot at the goal.

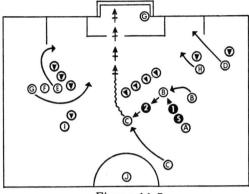

Figure 11-5

Purpose—This is a free kick used to draw the defenders toward the ball.

Drill 11-6 Thru the Hole

No. of players—Two full teams

Explanation—A passes the ball through the opening to player B. B should run close to the defenders on his left side to receive the ball on his right side.

Purpose—Player B overlaps and comes from the rear for a shot at the goal.

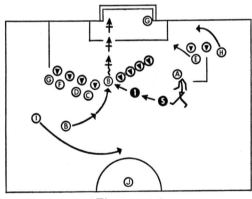

Figure 11-6

Drill 11-7 Screen the Wall

No. of players—Two full teams

Explanation—B starts his run. When B approaches D, D moves

to a position inside the gap in the wall. C and E make decoy runs. A passes to B. D must be careful to keep moving so he won't be called for obstructing the defender on the corner of the wall.

Purpose—Players make decoy runs to confuse the defenders.

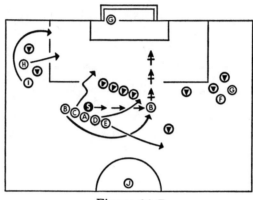

Figure 11-7

Drill 11-8 Over the Wall

No. of players—Two full teams

Explanation—B runs toward the ball and steps over it. B continues his run along the left side of the wall. A chips to B, who is on the run. B attempts to take the ball off his chest and volley on net.

Purpose—Players practice a maneuver used to get the ball behind the wall.

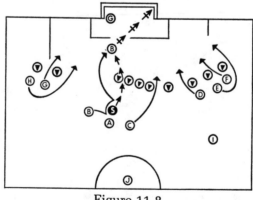

Figure 11-8

Drill 11-9 Either Side

No. of players—Two full teams

Explanation—C runs around the ball to the right while B runs around the ball to the left. A passes to either C or B depending on which player has a clear path to the goal.

Purpose—This pattern is used to surprise and confuse the defenders.

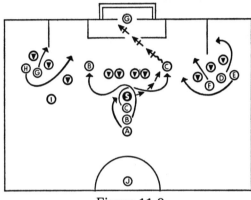

Figure 11-9

Drill 11-10 Double Wall

No. of players—Two full teams

Explanation—Players line up as seen in the diagram. A passes to B and B shoots at the goal. F is used to make the defenders think the ball will be played to him. G, H, and I line up in a manner so

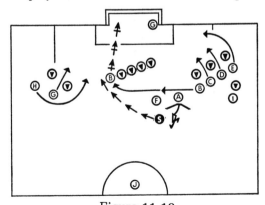

Figure 11-10

as to draw the defenders away from the area where the ball will be played.

Purpose—This is a way of stationing players to open a gap on the side of the wall.

Drill 11-11 Going Behind a Wall

No. of players—Two full teams

Explanation—A passes to B and B then passes behind the ball. D comes through for a shot.

Purpose—This is a maneuver used to pass the ball behind the wall.

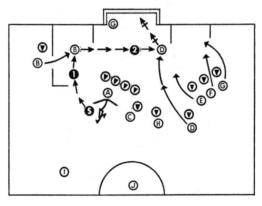

Figure 11-11

Figure 11-12

Drill 11-12 Through the Legs

No. of players—Two full teams

Explanation—A walks to the ball and pretends he is going to pick it up with his hands. Instead, he kicks it through B's legs to C. C kicks it to the left side of the wall. D comes from behind to take a shot at the goal.

Purpose—This maneuver is used to make the defense think the ball will be played to the right of the wall, while it is actually played to the left side of the wall.

Drill 11-13 Right and Left Gap

No. of players—Two full teams

Explanation—Players line up as seen in the diagram. This lineup is designed so that the opposition will be forced to leave gaps on either side of the wall. Player A signals for the other players to move toward the target areas shown in the diagram. Player A passes the ball through the gap. Where A decides to pass the ball depends on how the opposition lines up.

Purpose—This lineup is used to create gaps in the defense.

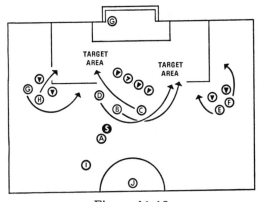

Figure 11-13

IV

TRAINING GAMES

Competitive training games are used to reinforce and to improve techniques and tactics. These activities are also used to help players to overcome deficiencies that might be evident in match play. In other words, they are sometimes used as troubleshooting tools. These games can provide specific and frequent encounters that are necessary for learning to occur.

In setting up and choosing a game, there are certain questions a coach should consider. They are:

What size should the playing area be?

How many players and goalkeepers are needed?

What equipment is needed—number of balls, number of goals, number and placement of area markers (cones), pinnies, etc.

What rules should be established?

What restrictions should be placed on the players?

What advantages can one of the teams be given to increase learning?

How long should the game be to produce the desired results?

How close is the action of the game to the action of match-playing conditions?

Is the technical or tactical objective of the game clear to the players?

What can be done to motivate players to participate with enthusiasm?

Training games are used to emphasize various phases of technique, tactics, and fitness. These games should simulate game-like conditions. Each game has an objective. This objective is reinforced by frequent repetition of game-like encounters. A full team scrimmage cannot provide enough reinforcement, repetition, and frequent encounters for economical learning. Therefore a coach should use small-sided games to accomplish this need.

These games enable a coach to concentrate on specific phases of the game that need attention. A coach can accomplish this by restricting the number of players, by adding or subtracting playing conditions, and by increasing or decreasing the size and/or shape of the playing area. The variations that a coach introduces should bring about the desired changes.

Many of these games are vigorous in nature and cause players to fatigue quickly. When the intent of the coach is to improve skill if he notices that the players are showing signs of fatigue, he should give them frequent rest periods. Skill deteriorates when players are fatigued and very little benefit is obtained when fatigue is present. On the other hand, when the objective of the coach is to improve the endurance or the general fitness of his players, he can continue these games for longer periods of time. The intensity and the objective of these games have a bearing on how long the game should or should not be continued.

It is frequently necessary for a coach to alter a game in order to reach his particular objective for that game. For example, while playing a half field keep away game of five vs. four, designed to teach players how to capitalize on numerical advantage situations, if a coach notices that frequent encounters to develop numerical advantage situations are not occurring, he can change the game. He can reduce the number of players on the team of four players, thus playing five vs. three. This change should help to increase the number and frequency of encounters and the number of numerical advantage situations encountered. Other alterations to these games can be used to increase and decrease the frequency of specific action. It is up to the coach to decide how and when he can use these alterations to accomplish his objective.

The games in this chapter were selected to offer a variety of activities that emphasize improving specific phases of the game of soccer.

12

Small-Sided Games
and Team Games

There are many variations that can be introduced into a game to emphasize different facets of soccer. Some of these variations would never be practiced unless special attention was called to them. The following are some of these variations:

Limiting players to 1 and 2 touches of the ball.

Playing a game where a player cannot pass to the player that passed to him.

Limiting or lengthening the distance a pass can be sent.

Playing with no goals, with two goals, or with four goals.

Playing a game in which only passes on the ground are permitted.

Playing a game in which only air passes are permitted.

Playing a game in which players can use only their weak feet to.pass the ball.

Playing a game in which the player who is passing must call out the name of the player who is receiving the pass.

Sometimes a combination of two or more of these variations can be used in the same game. There are many more variations of games than the ones mentioned above. These are only examples.

The selection of the variations of games is the coach's responsibility. His selections are based on the needs of his players that are evident from how they perform in match play.

Drill 12-1 Attack and Defend

No. of players—Two per drill group

Area of play—Inside the penalty area

Explanation—Four balls are placed inside the penalty area, as seen in the diagram. On a whistle, A sprints to the nearest ball and attempts to score a goal. The defender tries to prevent A from scoring. When a defender clears a ball out of the penalty area or when the attacker scores a goal, players quickly change roles. The attacker becomes the defender and the defender becomes the attacker. The new defender must wait until the new attacker touches the next ball before he attempts to make the tackle.

Purpose—Players practice quick changes from attacking to defending and from defending to attacking.

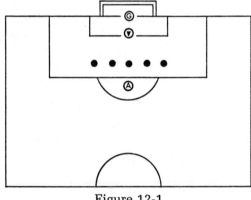

Figure 12-1

Drill 12-2 "1-Touch" Shooting Game (No Diagram)

No. of players—Two full teams

Area of play—A forty-yard by forty-yard square with goals at each end

Explanation—A regulation game of soccer is played. However, all shots at the goal are restricted to a "1-touch" shooting.

Purpose—Players practice "1-touch" shooting.

Drill 12-3 Five vs. Five in the Penalty Area (No Diagram)

No. of players—Ten per game

Equipment—A supply of soccer balls

Explanation—Four defenders and a goalkeeper play against five attackers inside the penalty area, the coach throws another ball into play to any unguarded attacking player.

Purpose—The objective is to practice quick and frequent shots at the goal.

Drill 12-4 Back Pass and Shoot (No Diagram)

No. of players—Two full teams

Explanation—Two full teams play a regular game of soccer. However, only shots taken from a back pass count in the scoring.

Purpose—Players practice back passing. Players learn to back pass rather than force the ball through the defense.

Drill 12-5 Hand and Head Ball (No Diagram)

No. of players—Unlimited

Explanation—Two teams of equal number participate in this game. It is played on half of a soccer field with two goals.

The game is played like team handball. However, players can only score by heading the ball into the goal. Players throw and catch the ball with their hands. Once a player catches a ball, he is restricted to three steps and then he must pass it off.

Purpose—This is a change-of-pace, fun activity. Players practice heading at the goal.

Drill 12-6 Passing Contest (No Diagram)

No. of players—Two full teams

Equipment—Each team has a ball.

Area of play—Half of a soccer field

Explanation—Two teams of an equal number of players compete to see which team can make the greatest number of passes in a specified time. This is done within the confines of the penalty area. Each team has its own ball.

Players of one team are not permitted to interfere with the passing of the other team, nor is a player permitted to pass back to the player who passed to him. Each pass must be at least five yards long.

Purpose—Players practice quick and accurate passing in a crowded area.

Drill 12-7 Advantage (No Diagram)

No. of players—Nine per game

Explanation—On half of a soccer field, using cones for goals at each end of the playing area, the following game of six versus three is played. The team with six players is restricted to "1-touch" play. The team of three has no restrictions on the number of touches.

Purpose—The team that has six players practices taking advantage of numerical advantage situations. The players should be encouraged to capitalize on these situations quickly.

Drill 12-8 Out or In (No Diagram)

No. of players—Three per drill group

Area of play—Inside the penalty area

Explanation—Five balls are placed inside the penalty area line. On a signal (whistle), A tries to get balls into the goal. The defender tries to kick the balls out of the penalty area. Play is completed when all balls are out of the penalty area or are inside the goal. One ball at a time is played by both players. Play starts when the attacker touches the first ball. When a defender wins the ball and kicks it out of bounds or a goal is scored, the attacker moves to attack with a new ball. The attacking player can fake playing one ball and then quickly move to attack with another. The defender should position himself between the ball and the goal until the attacker touches a ball.

Purpose—This is an intense game for both the attacker and the defender. Players learn not to relax after a play. Play is continuous and strenuous.

Drill 12-9 One-On-One Steal the Bacon

No. of players—Four per drill group

Area of play—Twenty- by twenty-yard square

Explanation—Play starts when the ball is kicked to the center of the square by the coach. A and B try to get control of the ball and attack their respective goals as seen in the diagram.

Purpose—Players practice open field dribbling and defending.

Variation—Add one more A player and one more B player to each team. Place these two players on the two vacant corners of the square, the B player on the bottom right of the square and A player on the top left corner of the square.

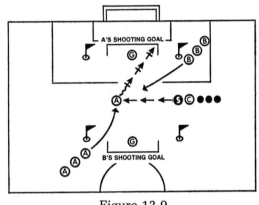

Figure 12-9

Drill 12-10 Short Pass Contest

No. of players—Six per team

Distance—See the diagram—All players are ten yards apart.

Explanation—On a signal (whistle), two teams compete to see which

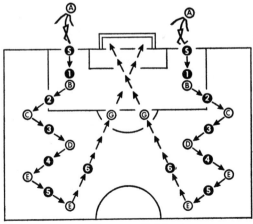

Figure 12-10

can pass a ball in the shortest period of time from A to G as seen in the diagram. The game is completed when G shoots at the goal.

Purpose—Players practice accurate, quick passing.

Drill 12-11 Look Up (No Diagram)

No. of players—Five-on-five or six-on six

Area—Half of a regular playing field

Explanation—A game of "1 touch", and "2-touch" or multiple touch is played on half of a regular playing field. No goals are used in this game. No colored shirts or pinnies are used to designate on what team each player is playing. This forces players to look up carefully before they pass the ball. No calling for the ball is permitted, so players must further rely on looking up before they pass the ball. Players rely on their memories to distinguish players assigned to their team.

Purpose—Players practice looking up and surveying the field before making a pass.

Drill 12-12 Draw Out (No Diagram)

No. of players—Five defenders and six attackers

Area of play—One-half of a soccer field

Explanation—A regular game of soccer is played on half of a soccer playing field. Play is started when one of the attacking team kicks the ball forward from the center circle. The main idea of this game is to draw defenders out and then play the ball behind them. To ensure the defenders will come out and mark attackers, introduce the rule that five consecutive passes by the attacking team constitutes a goal.

The coach should stress that the ball must move quickly and it should be played on the ground. The attacking team is instructed to exert patience and not to force the ball. When play gets jammed up, players are instructed to play the ball back and start a new attack.

Purpose—This game teaches players to practice patience and to wait for the defense to make a mistake. Encourage attackers to make blind side runs, decoy runs, overlapping runs, and, when they get bogged down, to play the ball back to start another attack.

Drill 12-13 Air Ball (No Diagram)

No. of players—Six on six

Explanation—The game is played in an area forty yards by forty yards. Four goals are situated in the middle of each of the four sidelines. A supply of balls should be kept ready to put into play.

Play starts when one player from team A kicks a ball dropped from his hands. From this time on, the ball is played in the air. When it hits the ground, it is given to team B. Play starts again when the player from team B drops the ball and kicks it. Shots can be taken at any of the four goals by members of either team.

Purpose—Players practice playing a ball in the air, as well as taking volley shots at the goal.

Drill 12-14 Four Plus Six vs. Four

No. of players—Fourteen per game

Explanation—As and Bs play a game of keep-away within the confines of the penalty area. The team in possession of the ball can pass to any C player. C players are restricted to "1-touch" passing. C players are restricted to staying outside the penalty area, but are permitted to move around anywhere outside the penalty area line.

Purpose—Players practice passing, receiving, and controlling. Players practice "1-touch" wall passes with the C players.

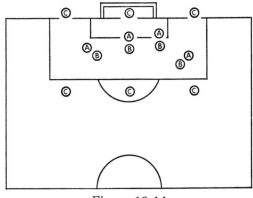

Figure 12-14

Drill 12-15 Six-on-Seven (Half field) (No Diagram)

No. of players—Thirteen per game.

Area of play—Half of a regular playing field.

Explanation—The defensive team has seven players, six field players, and one goalkeeper. The attacking team has six field players.

The game is played like a regular game only the attacking team scores by putting the ball in the goal and the defensive team scores by making five consecutive passes. Play is continuous. If the defensive team makes ten consecutive passes in a row, this is counted as two goals. When a ball goes out of bounds or over the center line, it is brought back in play by the regular throw-in. When the ball goes over the endline, it is treated like a corner kick or a six-yard kick, depending on which player touches it last. All passses back to the goalkeeper are counted toward the five passes, but the goalkeeper is restricted to handling these passes only with his feet.

Purpose—Players practice offensive and defensive skills. The attacking players practice winning the ball back once it is lost or intercepted. Attacking players should be encouraged to pursue the ball immediately once it is lost.

Drill 12-16 Patience (No Diagram)

No. of players—Ten on ten (No Goalkeeper)

Area of play—Full soccer field

Explanation—Divide and mark off the field into three sections—the defensive third, the mid-field third, and the attacking third. No goals are scored in this game.

The ball is started by the goalkeeper in the defensive third for a period of time—one minute or more. The ball cannot be advanced until the coach blows the whistle. It can then be moved to the mid-field third. The attacking team continues to maintain possession of the ball in this section of the field for a period of one minute or more. The same procedure is then performed in the attack section of the field.

If the defending team wins possession of the ball, it is given back to the attacking team until they can maintain possession for a period of one minute in a particular section of the field.

After a team maintains possession in each of the three sections of the field for a period of one minute or more, the other team repeats the same procedure going in the opposite direction.

Purpose—The main purpose of this game is to practice maintaining possession of the ball in various sections of the field.

Drill 12-17 No Goal Soccer (No Diagram)

No. of players—Ten on ten

Area of play—Full field

Explanation—This game is played like a regular game only there is no shooting. The objective of this game is for an attacking team to successfully pass a ball into the goal area. The same team can score two or more times in a row by passing the ball out of the goal area and then passing it back into the goal area.

Purpose—Players concentrate on passing skills without worrying about shooting at the goal.

Drill 12-18 Win Back (No Diagram)

No. of players—Two full teams

Area of play—One half of a regular soccer field

Explanation—The idea behind this game is to get all team members to concentrate on defense once the ball is lost. It is played on half of the field.

Play starts when the goalkeeper from team A rolls the ball to a teammate. A team members then try to get the ball over a line through the center of the field. The A team is limited to short passes (ten to fifteen yards) to accomplish this task. The B team tries to prevent the A team from crossing the one-half field line. When B team intercepts or wins the ball, it starts an immediate attack on the goal. In this case, A team members become defenders. When the B team looses the ball or scores a goal, play is started again with A's goalkeeper rolling out another ball. Also, if the A team is successful in crossing the center line with the ball, play is started after players resume their original positions. Then A's goalkeeper rolls out another ball and play begins again.

Purpose—Players practice an all-out effort to win the ball back in their opponents defensive area of the field. Players practice and develop a quick counterattack.

Drill 12-19 Four Team Soccer (No Diagram)

No. of players—Four teams of five players on each team plus a goalkeeper

Area of play—One half of a regular soccer field with goals at each end

Equipment—A different colored shirt for each team and two soccer balls.

Explanation—Two games of soccer are played on half of a soccer field at the same time. Each team has a different colored shirt. For example: red team and green team attack one goal and blue team and yellow team attack another goal. Red plays against blue and green plays against yellow. The red and blue teams do not interfere with the green and yellow game and vice versa.

Purpose—Players learn to get their heads up before passing the ball. Players learn the fundamentals of ball control in a congested situation.

Drill 12-20 Counterattack—Defense (No Diagram)

No. of players—Two full teams

Explanation—A regular game of soccer is played, except that when a whistle is blown teams reverse roles. The team in possession of the ball quickly (on the whistle) runs and attacks the opposite goal. The defending team must quickly run to the other end of the field and set up a defense. The goalkeepers do not change goals. They defend against whichever team is attacking their goals. Defenders attempt to contain the attack until they can set up.

This game is very tiring so the coach should be realistic about the number of times the whistle is blown for players to change ends of the field.

Purpose—Players practice quickly changing ends of the field that they are defending and attacking. Defenders practice recovering and quickly setting up on the other end of the field. Attackers practice breaking up counterattacks.

Drill 12-21 Three-on-two—Wing Play

No. of players—Five per drill group

Explanation—In a fifteen-yard corridor along the sidelines, as seen in the diagram, three attackers play against two defenders. Play starts at mid-field. A score occurs when the attacking players make four consecutive passes inside the square marked off in the area at the far end of the field. When a score occurs (four consecutive passes inside the square), play is stopped. Players walk back to mid-field and begin again.

When the defenders win possession of the ball, play is restarted at mid-field.

Purpose—Players practice working the ball to the corner area in a numerical advantage situation.

Variation—In order to speed up the attack, add a third defender who starts on the goalline behind the attackers. The third defender comes into play when the attacking team crosses over the middle line.

Purpose of the variation—The variation is used to make the attacking team speed up its attack. The attacking team must speed up the attack to preserve its numerical superiority.

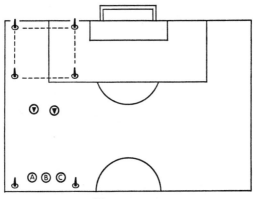

Figure 12-21

Drill 12-22 No Trespassing

No. of players—Two full teams

Equipment—Eight cones or flags. Four cones are placed on each half of the field to mark off a twenty-yard square, as seen in the diagram.

Explanation—A regular full team game is played. Players are not permitted to enter the "No Trespass" area. They can pass the ball through this area but they cannot step inside it.

Purpose—This game forces players to use the wing area when attacking.

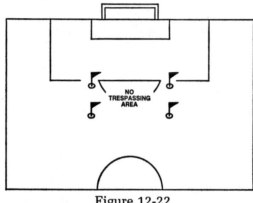

Figure 12-22

Index

H

I

K

L

M